Be kind to yourself

A 52-Week Workbook
to Nurture Your *Beautiful Self*
through the Good Times, the Messy Times,
and *All the Seasons In Between*

Be Kind to Yourself

A 52-Week Workbook
to Nurture Your *Beautiful Self*
through the Good Times, the Messy Times,
and *All the Seasons In Between*

MEGAN LOGAN, MSW, LCSW

BETTER DAY BOOKS®

HAPPY · CREATIVE · CURATED

DEDICATION

For "Old Girl," the beautiful cherry tree that inspired this book.
May she continue to grow and change in all her glory through the seasons of life.

Be Kind to Yourself © 2022 by Megan Logan and Better Day Books, Inc.

Publisher: Peg Couch
Editor: Colleen Dorsey
Book Designer: Michael Douglas
Cover Designer: Dawn Nicole Warnaar
Additional design elements by Dawn Nicole Warnaar on pages
4, 6, 7, 12, 13, 151, orange flowers (throughout), week number
decorations (throughout), and the back cover.

Library of Congress Control Number: 2022935407

ISBN: 978-0-7643-6546-1

Printed in China

First printing

Copublished by Better Day Books, Inc., and Schiffer Publishing, Ltd.

Better Day Books
P.O. Box 21462
York, PA 17402
Phone: 717-487-5523
Email: hello@betterdaybooks.com
www.betterdaybooks.com
@better_day_books

Schiffer Publishing
4880 Lower Valley Road
Atglen, PA 19310
Phone: 610-593-1777
Fax: 610-593-2002
Email: info@schifferbooks.com
www.schifferbooks.com

This title is available for promotional or commercial use,
including special editions. Contact info@schifferbooks.com
for more information.

Acknowledgments

My sister in Pennsylvania has a big and beautiful old cherry tree in her backyard. We call her "Old Girl." I'm always in awe of her glory as she transforms each season — covered white with snow, to blossoming pink petals and alive with green leaves, to finally ablaze with the fire of autumn. "Old Girl" became the inspiration for *Be Kind to Yourself,* as the workbook follows each season. This beautiful tree taught me to be kind to myself and embrace growth and change with grace through the many cycles in my beautiful, crazy, and sometimes messy life. Each season brings with it a reason to celebrate, whether recharging in the colder months, rebirthing with the springtime, embracing life through summer, or letting go in the fall.

A special thanks to the many clients I have worked with through the years who have shown me the importance of nurturing the body, mind, spirit, and the world around and within us. I am honored to play a small part in your nurturing journey and hope the reflections and exercises help renew and restore you.

Contents

START WHERE YOU ARE

Track your self-love journey by checking off each week as you complete it! You can start in any season or jump around from week to week if desired — do what works for you.

WINTER: Rest and Nurture

SPRING: Awaken and Grow

SUMMER: Play and Explore

FALL: Reflect and Let Go

Hello!

I'm so glad you found this book! My name is Megan Logan, and I am a licensed clinical social worker and the bestselling author of *Self-Love Workbook for Women*. After publishing my first book, I realized I still had so much I wanted to give, which led to the book you're now holding in your hands.

Here's a little info about me. I received a bachelor's degree in Social Work with a minor in Family Issues from James Madison University in Virginia, and, later, I received my master's degree in Clinical Social Work from Florida State University. For the last 22 years, I have provided mental health therapy in a variety of settings, including domestic violence and sexual assault centers, foster care agencies, community-based mental health programs, hospices, and, currently, private practice. In my practice, I specialize in issues related to trauma and abuse, eating disorders, grief and loss, and play therapy.

My work has been featured in the *Chicago Tribune, Rolling Stone Magazine,* and *Elle Magazine UK*. I've recently started to widen my healing practice by becoming a Master Reiki Practitioner, and I'm studying to become a crystal sound bowl practitioner—I truly love learning new techniques to provide the most effective and holistic healing for others.

I'm originally from Annapolis, Maryland, but I currently live in St. Augustine, Florida, where I like searching for shark's teeth on the beach—though one day I hope to live in the mountains. I also enjoy spending time with my two awesome teenagers and learning from them what true motherhood means.

I hope with all my heart that you learn and grow as you take your own journey through this book and a year's worth of deep, personal reflection. I'd love to hear from you! Check me out at *www.meganloganlcsw.com* and on Instagram @meganloganlcsw, and feel free to drop me a line.

XO Megan

Introduction

Depleted. Exhausted. Overcommitted. If you're like me, life has become filled with endless energy drainers, often leading to disconnection and distraction. Scrambling around from one event to the next, a constant attachment to our cell phones, and checking off an endless to-do list can leave us feeling burned out, worn down, and unfulfilled.

I sometimes long for the days of the answering machine when work stayed at work until the next morning and weekends provided a nice little break from life. I'm not sure about you, but my weekends have become filled with the things I don't have time to complete during the week, like grocery shopping, housecleaning, and yard work. As a sports family, we spend our weekends on the pitch, with sometimes up to eight games — all to turn around and go to school and work on Monday. There is no day off. No wonder I'm exhausted and feeling slightly burned out! If you're like me, finding time for nurturing anything, much less yourself, seems like a luxury.

I think back to thirty years ago when my church youth group would take almost a hundred teenagers on a weekend retreat twice a year. I was always excited for this time with friends surrounded by scenic mountains or next to a beautiful lake. I came away rested, rejuvenated, and reconnected to my faith and friends. It was the perfect fall and spring reset, and I am so lucky to have had this privilege for six years of my developmental foundation. I can't imagine having social media to compete with or missing this opportunity to learn the value of rest at such a young age. Even now, I daydream about having a retreat center with my sisters called Three Sisters Retreat, a place for spiritual, physical, and emotional healing. But let's be honest, we'd probably kill each other, and it's best not to go into business with family.

While nurturing my dream of something larger and beyond the scope of providing therapy, the *Be Kind to Yourself* workbook came into existence. I envision this book will serve as a guide to nurturing your mind, body, and spirit. I like to think of it as a retreat in and of itself. Through weekly reflection, prompts, and exercises organized by the seasons, come embark on a journey filled with nurturing meant to replenish your heart and mind. I am honored you have chosen this book to accompany your quest for nurturing.

Reflecting Before Beginning

Before starting our journey together, let's take a quick glimpse into your current beliefs about extending kindness to yourself through nurturing practices. Consider each statement and notice your reactions. Which ones feel impossible or uncomfortable, and which ones excite you or make you want to explore more? You can come back to this list after completing the book and see how you've changed.

- I enjoy finding ways to nurture my mind, body, and spirit.
- I nurture myself on a regular basis.
- I practice loving kindness to myself and the world around me.
- I nurture myself in many different ways.
- I embrace my inner god/goddess and know how to share them in the world.
- Practicing kindness to myself helps me to extend that same kindness to others.
- Extending kindness to myself through nurturing involves intention and hard work.
- I am excited to start reflecting on ways to be kinder to myself.
- I feel overwhelmed with where to start.
- I believe it will be hard to find time to do this workbook.

52 Weeks of Nurturing

This book explores weekly topics about nurturing designed to speak to your heart and inspire a change in your life. Divided into four segments aligning with the seasons of both nature and life, each chapter highlights different themes like goal-setting and values clarification, rebirth and dreaming, mindfully living in the moment, and letting go and releasing what no longer serves you. This workbook journey delves into both light and darkness, bringing feelings of rawness, inspiration, and magic when fully embraced.

This book is designed to be a personal exploration, but you can also use it through sharing with others. Perhaps complete the exercises with your support tribe, as an adjunct to therapy, or as part of a virtual book club. Sharing your unique perspective and insights in a group adds richness to the experience and is a wonderful way to nurture ourselves and others simultaneously. Check out more ideas for using this book in a group on page 237.

The practical exercises and quizzes throughout this book are designed for introspection and reflection, and they are based on my more than twenty years of experience as a therapist. They are uniquely developed from evidenced-based theoretical models of counseling. However, they are not professional diagnostic tools or validated through specific, dedicated research.

Start where you are.

You don't have to start with Winter, Week 1. Feel free to open the book and choose any chapter that speaks to you. The exercises have been grouped together to reflect each season's theme, but each exercise can exist independently. It is also okay to skip an exercise if it doesn't resonate with you.

WINTER ❮ Rest and Nurture

Winter is full of opportunities for rest and nurturing that are often hidden amongst the chilly air, long nights, and snowy whiteness. It is a time for curling up with a cup of hot chocolate and getting cozy by the fireplace with loved ones. The cold darkness of winter allows for deeper rest and hibernation, a chance for our brains and bodies to recharge and reflect upon the upcoming new year. Come, rest with me, and nurture this season of winter.

SPRING ❮ Awaken and Grow

As new life awakens from the thawing land and little creatures begin to delight in the growing daylight hours, spring inspires renewal and a blossoming of creativity, innocence, love, and hope. Brighter, longer days shine amidst blooming flowers while singing lovebirds call out, "Spring is here!" Showers, raining down magical blessings, create new life and a rainbow of new beginnings and possibilities. Come, grow with me, and nurture this season of spring.

SUMMER ❮ Play and Explore

This is a time for frolicking in the bright warmth and enjoying the sunny blessings in our lives. Summertime involves dreams of running barefoot through the green grass surrounded by bright blue sky or along the sandy shore, gathering Mother Nature's trinkets and treasures. Summer unlocks the freedom to explore the adventures of life, delights with happy squeals of joy, and sunbeams and fresh air. Come, play with me, and nurture this season of summer.

FALL ❮ Reflect and Let Go

Beautiful colors blaze through the cool wilderness as the trees release what no longer serves them. Dusk begins to fall, and darkness creeps in while change infiltrates, calling for preparation and deeper reflection. Leaves falling to the ground make way for the harvest of gratitude. Abundance grows to maturity while we learn to let go and reflect on the natural cycles of life and loss. Come, let go with me, and nurture this season of fall.

Silence for Noisy Hearts

*The quieter you become,
the more you are able to hear.*

— RUMI

So often, we run around pulled in many directions, our hearts stretched to capacity as we try to balance multiple internal and external demands. Interpersonal relationships and responsibilities may lead to uncomfortable emotions. These worries, often centered around the people we care about and situations or events outside of our control, tend to fill up our heart space, leaving little room for inner peace.

Now, zoom farther out and consider the larger community, the national and worldwide arena. Some events around us, like pandemics, mass shootings, interpersonal violence, political unrest, injustice, and war, may provoke strong emotions and reactions as they touch upon basic needs like shelter, food, clothing, safety, finances, and health. Our hearts can fill with a cacophony of endless congestion that sometimes feels heavy and overwhelming. This pileup becomes particularly daunting for those that lean toward the compassionate, empathic side.

When filled with the clanging internal and external chatter of the world around and within us, nurturing silence becomes an essential skill. Yes, you can learn to create a moment of inner peace by developing a regular mindfulness practice.

Have you ever tried to allow yourself space and time to sit in the present moment without moving to change or fix something? For some, this can feel uncomfortable and strange. But sitting in a room where there is little noise or distraction might happen more easily than shutting off the endless chatter in our minds. One of the quickest ways to find mindfulness and work toward nurturing inner quiet involves allowing yourself permission to simply be — without judging yourself or the moment. This involves noticing and observing through the five senses and awareness of the thoughts in your mind that might distract you from your task of simply being in the moment.

One of my favorite experiences for practicing solitude involved a silent retreat. In my mid-twenties, I attended a spiritual development group called Nurturing Silence in Noisy Hearts — a weekly meeting for silent journaling and reflection. This group ended with a silent retreat where we spent the weekend with no talking. We journaled and enjoyed the mountain scenery, spending time alone for silent reflection. While not everyone can attend a silent retreat weekend getaway, it can be helpful to develop a plan for nurturing silence. What would you think about a silent weekend with no talking to others?

Turning off the chatter in our minds can feel impossible. If you're like me, it seems

Five Quick Ways to Nurture Silence in Noisy Hearts

1. Do something crafty, like color, or create a collage expressing your feelings.

2. Try journaling your feelings without censoring yourself to release and make space for new.

3. Stop and tune in to your five senses by practicing mindfulness. Just notice and become aware of what you see, smell, taste, touch, and hear in this moment.

4. Breathe. Focus on each inhalation or exhalation. I like triangle breathing: Breathe in while you count to five, hold while you count to five, exhale while you count to five. You can even draw a triangle and trace the sides with your finger as you breathe in and out.

5. Unplug. Turn off electronics and tune in to your surroundings. I have had to actually put my phone in my vehicle to keep from using it!

like a thousand thoughts race through your brain each minute. But while you cannot always stop thoughts from happening, realizing a thought is just a thought is a game-changer. You do not need to give energy to the thought, analyze it from all angles, or attach meaning to it. A thought becomes simply words strung together in the mind. Notice the thought and let it pass through the gates of meaning and interpretation. When stuck at the gate of analysis, thoughts pile up, causing a traffic jam; but allowing thoughts to pass through without stopping makes way for internal silence.

When hearts and minds become saturated with internal and external noise, practicing mindfulness allows us to find our center — without fixing, numbing, hiding, or distracting. An intentional way to practice begins with mindfulness by simply noticing our thoughts. *It does not require silence to nurture silence in a noisy heart.* Simple awareness of a thought, feeling, or sensation passing through without applying meaning and interpretation allows for silence. The trapping creates the noise, not the thought itself.

How to Navigate Through a Traffic Jam in Our Minds

1. Observe any thoughts you have parked in your brain. (Example: "This exercise is stupid.")

2. Notice yourself noticing you having this thought. (Example: "I'm aware that I'm having the thought 'this exercise is stupid'.")

3. Pay attention to any judgment or meaning placed on this situation (good, bad, stupid, smart). Judgment creates a new feeling or thought and leads to more congestion.

4. Notice the thought is just words.

5. Repeat to yourself, "Interesting, the thought 'this exercise is stupid' just popped into my head."

6. You don't have to do anything with this thought; just notice and observe it.

My Noisy Heart

For this exercise, let's identify the internal and external noises weighing heavily on your heart. Reflect for a moment on things in your life that create noise. Consider the world around you, and then look deeper to identify those places within you that stir up chatter in your mind — perhaps injustice, unfairness, or personal insecurities. Inside the heart below, write or draw those burdens. Outside the heart, identify those external struggles that add to the noise in your heart.

Now take time to just notice and observe what you shared. Try practicing the mindfulness skills described previously, and apply these skills to your filled-in heart. Notice and observe any emotions or body sensations.

Solitude for Crowded Hearts

*I find it wholesome to be alone
the greater part of the time. Even with the best,
being in company is soon wearisome and dissipating.
I love to be alone. I never found the companion
that was so companionable as solitude.*

— HENRY DAVID THOREAU, *Walden*

Have you ever felt lonely while surrounded by other people or been alone and not felt lonely? The terms "lonely" and "alone" differ, with the first offering a feeling of rejection and the second consisting simply of spending time by oneself.

Interestingly, the meaning attached to solitude makes a difference in the experience of it. Depending on your personality, you may gain or lose energy from time spent alone, or you may become energized or drained when interacting with others.

Regardless, nurturing solitude allows for reflection, introspection, and a chance to tune into our inner world. In my early twenties, I believed I was weird because I didn't want to go to parties in college or hang out socially. Living in an extroverted world, I felt pressure to be more social and engage in activities that

I found draining and just not enjoyable. Eventually, I learned that there was nothing wrong with me for wanting to spend quiet evenings in my pajamas reading a book. I was just an introvert! In fact, I needed this downtime and space to allow myself time to recharge my battery.

Too much solitude, though, drives disconnection. Depending on everyone's individual needs, solitude must find a way to balance with life. A closer look at our personal values in a future chapter will help clarify the competing priorities in life.

Think for a moment about solitude and what it means for you to be alone. What images come to mind? What colors do you see, and how does it make you feel? When do you find yourself needing solitude, and how do you incorporate this into your busy life?

Last year I took a solo trip to Asheville, North Carolina, to enjoy kayaking down the French Broad River and hiking in the Appalachians. I spent time at a few little shops and enjoyed eating alone at small cafés, feeling rested, restored, and enjoying only the sounds of nature and my own thoughts. This time of solitude didn't feel lonely at all. It felt like heaven for me, a much-needed respite from the crazy world and time to renew and restore my energy.

Consider for a moment how you might feel on a solo weekend getaway. Would this feel comfortable for you? Why or why not?

Assess Yourself: A Time for Solitude?

Fill in the clock in the style of a pie chart with time spent during your average day, including all the basic activities like sleep and work, plus things like mealtimes, exercise, movies, etc. Notice during which activities nurturing solitude happens. For me, it is mostly when I am sleeping!

Solitude offers a chance for nurturing time alone and enjoying the company of ourselves. For some people, time alone feels wonderfully relaxing, and for others, it can feel quite stressful and uncomfortable. The world's recent call for quarantining due to the pandemic highlights this perfectly. Think for a moment about how you managed during quarantine. As an introvert, I personally enjoyed the quiet time and isolation as it allowed me to slow down, work from home, and write my first book. Others I know felt uncomfortable and drained by not socializing with people, triggering feelings of loneliness and isolation.

Whether you lean more towards introversion or extroversion, though, everyone can benefit from solitude.

It is difficult to talk about solitude without addressing loneliness. When feeling lonely and hurting, I have learned to shift my focus and flip the meaning of this emotion to provide an opportunity for self-nurturing by engaging in self-care activities I enjoy. When in solitude, whether by choice or circumstance, it can help to have a plan for filling time and space with something meaningful and to reframe this experience as an opportunity for self-care.

My Solitude Kit

Make yourself a Solitude Kit stocked with things to do when you find yourself alone. This can provide a wonderful way to nurture solitude no matter where you fit along the introversion-extroversion scale.

Here's my sample Solitude Kit:

- Mud mask/bath or shower bombs
- Journaling
- Music
- Netflix or a movie
- Camera
- Colored pencils and coloring books

Creating a Space for Solitude

In this exercise, draw the ideal place for nurturing solitude. Consider the details in the surroundings and reflect on what makes this place perfect for solitude and reflection.

If you find yourself unable to create a real place, feel free to create an imaginary place. Perhaps it's somewhere you've never actually been, or even a fantasy world. When using imagery, try focusing on the sensory details that exist. Be sure to include what you see, smell, taste, feel, and hear! One of my favorite things to do when I'm alone and nurturing solitude involves daydreaming and creating places or situations that make me feel calm, relaxed, or joyful.

Hibernation for Weary Souls

*I have a sequence to my creative life. In spring
and fall, I am above ground and commit to community.
In the summer, I'm outside. It is a time for family. And in
the winter, I am underground. Home. This is when I do
my work as a writer — in hibernation. I write with the bears.*

— TERRY TEMPEST WILLIAMS

Imagine a big, furry brown bear, seemingly slumbering in a dark, cold winter cave, surviving on his stored fat through the harsh winter months. Hibernation allows some animals to conserve energy through slower breathing and heart rates and decreased body temperature, allowing for survival.

Every winter, I jokingly say I wish I was a bear so I could hibernate after gorging myself all fall. No leg shaving, shoveling snow, or hustling and bustling with the holidays. Wouldn't it be nice to have a whole season of rest with no expectations but conserving the reserves? If you're like me, more time devoted to pure resting sounds heavenly. I'm not talking laziness and gluttony. I mean respite to restore the body and soul from the stressful conditions of modern life. Nope, hibernation isn't just for the bears.

Technically, hibernation doesn't mean slumber. It's more about survival and conserving energy. I believe humans could benefit from nurturing time for rest as a key component of self-care and rejuvenation. This particularly rings true because most of us spin around on the crazy merry-go-round of life, moving from one event to another with little time for rest and lots of time for stress. Technology keeps us plugged in and connected 24/7, while our workplace culture fosters burnout and exhaustion. While our ancestors experienced a different kind of stress with survival through the Great Depression and wartimes, I believe our modern world, while convenient and filled with luxuries, creates a different unnecessary stress that just might call for an evolutionary adaptation like a season of hibernation.

In what ways do you currently practice hibernation? Are there certain seasons in your life that allow for rest and retreat? School-aged children typically become conditioned to anticipate a winter break, a spring break, and a summer break during the school year. This morphs into a typical workweek by adulthood, allowing a day or two of "rest" at a time instead of an entire season. Add parenthood or caregiving to a job, and you have the beginnings of exhaustion.

With so much of our time focused on productivity, keeping up with others, or pursuing security, our worth has become tied to a never-ending chase for something better. If they're lucky,

most people get a couple of weeks of vacation. Not sure about you, but I want more time—a way to find meaning and balance with the simple joys in life and contribute to the world. This sentiment reflects my personal values, which are highly individualized and never right or wrong. Depending on your values, the desire for hibernation might change.

As a hospice social worker, part of my work involved engaging in informal life reviews with dying patients and their loved ones. What a sacred honor to share in someone's preparation as they make peace and plan for the transition from this world. It is a time for reflection on regrets, joys, moments of pride, and what they'd have done differently. Often I heard, "I would have enjoyed life more," "I would have spent more time with my family and less at work," "I would have worried less about stuff that doesn't matter." This is wisdom worth sharing for those seeking balance in work and life.

Reflection Time

If you found out that you had six months to live, what immediate changes would you make in your life? How would you choose to spend your remaining months? Would rest and relaxation become a part of the equation? What regrets would you have in your life related to how you spent your time?

Grinding away in our achievement-driven society can leave broken pieces and sometimes regrets. Examining how we spend large portions of our time — namely, working — can be a personal values clarification opportunity. This does not mean that prioritizing success, hard work, or achievement is automatically negative; but by reflecting on these things, we can push to find more meaning in life, balance, and increased self-awareness.

Clarifying values can help propel us forward when we feel stuck and are having difficulty finding ways to incorporate something new into our lives. Aligning our energy output in the world with our core values offers a chance to find fulfillment, meaning, and peace. While this does not necessitate a huge change in life circumstances, further exploration into our values can help clarify areas that might need change.

Values Inventory

Consider the values below and pick your top ten. How do the values you chose impact the idea of rest in your life?

Patriotism	Intelligence	Honesty	Love
Home	Humor	Prosperity	Passion
Community	Security	Fitness	Fun
Peace	Authenticity	Learning	Playfulness
Freedom	Simplicity	Wellness	Patience
Adventure	Fame	Harmony	Curiosity
Travel	Justice	Balance	Beauty
Respect	Courage	Friendships	The arts
Diversity	Compassion	Romance	Heritage
Creativity	Openness	Knowledge	Resilience
Humanity	Risks	Growth	Legacy
Wealth	Spirituality	Career	Loyalty
Integrity	Faith	Gratitude	Nature
Success	Teamwork	Grace	Family

Cozy Life

Fill in the house with ideas on creating more rest and relaxation. What would this look like, and how can you make it happen? Be creative, and if you struggle to find time to carve into your busy schedule, consider reassessing your values and what would need to change in your life to make space for restorative opportunities.

4

Stillness in Busy Minds

Look at a tree, a flower, a plant.
Let your awareness rest upon it. How still they are,
how deeply rooted in being.
Allow nature to teach you stillness.

— ECKHART TOLLE

So often, we find ourselves hustling and moving around our fast-paced lives, making peace and tranquility quite elusive. Nurturing calmness and stillness seems like a luxury reserved for Tibetan monks. The practice of creating inner peace must involve intentional dedication — it does not happen magically in our fast-paced, technologically driven world. Learning mindfulness and meditation allows for small moments of stillness that connect to larger moments, ultimately creating peace.

Having learned to meditate, I can now easily meditate anywhere, anytime, and anyplace. It took a lot of practice and feeling like it wasn't working before I eventually carved a pathway in my brain allowing for holding space in the present moment. That's the key word right there: practice. It is not going to work at first — your mind will wander, and you will lose focus.

I wouldn't expect you to run a 5K or a marathon if you lead a sedentary life and haven't worked out in ten years.

Keep focusing and practicing, and eventually, a few seconds will lead to minutes and then hours. Soon you'll be able to nurture calm on demand.

Nurturing calmness and stillness does not involve disconnecting and numbing. It means tuning into the moment and fostering a sense of peace, even when chaos might exist around or within us. Have you ever found yourself driving and not recalling how you got somewhere? While it might seem calming to drive on autopilot, this does not represent mindfulness but rather mild and often normal dissociation. True calmness and stillness come from being connected to our present moment with an ability to make space for peace.

A great way to start your journey and practice building the mindfulness muscle involves guided imageries, which are easy to find online. Eventually, mindfulness and meditation will become second nature and easier to apply to situations that might provoke strong emotions and reactions. Mindfulness can help allow uncomfortable feelings or situations, providing a vehicle to transcend beyond chaos by allowing and accepting the uncomfortable.

What challenges come up for you as you practice mindfulness? Do you find it hard to still and quiet your thoughts?

Float Like a Leaf

For this exercise, picture a stream flowing gently. Imagine a shiny and beautiful leaf gliding along the water, slowing moving with the current as the sunlight bathes the leaf in warmth and glistens on the sparkling water. Imagine birds chirping in the background and a soft breeze gently rustling in the trees along the stream. What would it feel like to be this leaf floating on a lazy stream with no cares in the world?

In the leaf below, fill in what this experience might feel like. During this mini-meditation, pay attention to what you see, smell, taste, touch, and hear.

Do you think it is a waste of time or that you could be more productive doing something else? Do distractions like pets, kids, or roommates around you interrupt your quiet?

Relaxing on a tropical island with a fruity drink, or indulging in a dimly lit bath surrounded by the soothing herbal smells of lavender and mint, might make it easier and more entertaining to practice mindfulness. But, sadly, these situations do not happen regularly, so mindfulness must be encouraged within common day-to-day experiences.

At the beginning of my mindfulness practice, I recall that I would struggle to relax even during a massage. My brain would think random thoughts about my day or worry that I might gross the massage therapist out with my cellulite or stubbly legs. The internal, most often negative, chatter worked endlessly to wreak havoc on my peaceful quiet. I had to learn to overcome those barriers more effectively by replacing my anxious thoughts with more helpful ones or just observing and noticing the thoughts without judgment while repeatedly bringing my attention back to the present sensations. Notice what barriers come up for you when evaluating a mindfulness practice so you can troubleshoot and find ways to address those blocks.

Mindfulness Hack

As a child, I loved looking out the window at the streetlight at night, watching giant snowflakes falling from the sky. Over and over, I would pick out one snowflake way up in the sky and follow it to the ground. Little did I know I was practicing mindfulness. A quick hack for learning mindfulness involves observing and describing a situation using your full senses.

Imagine that you step outside into a snowy winter wonderland. Describe the experience using your five senses.

Sight   Smell   Taste   Touch   Hearing

Building a
Mindfulness Practice

So how do you build a mindfulness practice into your life to create
calm stillness amidst the chaos? Consider for a moment what things keep you
busy in your life. When do you have time to nurture stillness and calm?
What in your environment allows for this? In this exercise, write about what
life looks like when busy and chaotic and then calm. What must change?

My Busy Life

Life Without Chaos and Busyness

What Had to Change

WEEK
5

Privacy for Public Lives

*Here in your mind you have
complete privacy. Here there's no difference
between what is and what could be.*

— CHUCK PALAHNIUK, *Choke*

Social media and technology allow us to stay plugged in and connected 24/7, sometimes making it feel like we're living in a fishbowl. For those more than thirty years old, it might feel strange to reminisce about the time before everyone knew what everyone else was doing at any given time and photos were only seen in albums or picture frames. For some, social media allows for staying connected with family and friends or finding support and inspiration. But social media can feel overwhelming and compelling at times, requiring us to post things about our day-to-day lives for the world to see.

Marketing and consumerism drive search engine optimization, creating a pattern and an electronic footprint tracked by big companies to pursue your business and turn a profit. Have you ever talked aloud about an item, and then it shows up on a computer-generated ad? Complete privacy can feel elusive, though we attempt to protect ourselves with private browsers and incognito search engines.

So, what is privacy exactly, and why is it so important in our society? The

Merriam-Webster dictionary defines privacy as "the quality or state of being apart from company or observation" and "freedom from unauthorized intrusion." The Latin term for privacy, *privatus*, means "set apart from what is public and belonging to oneself (not to the state)."

Consider for a moment how the word *private* shows up in our language. From private eyes and private property to private parts and private schools, our Western world values privacy, which has become synonymous with freedom.

Privacy as a human right allows us protection in the freedom to think, believe, and have different associations and affiliations. It ensures protection from overreaching intrusion in our lives and offers a sense of control.

As a therapist, nothing rings truer than the importance of protecting confidentiality. Creating safety for clients to openly share feelings and experiences is almost sacred. In working with children, I sometimes give them invisible ink pens to write in their journals or during sessions. This is a fun yet safe way to ensure that others won't see their deepest, most private thoughts and feelings.

Think for a moment about how privacy has shown up in your life. During the teenage years, privacy might mean having your own room, keeping a diary, or even having a fake Instagram account for teens today. As a young mother, I recall privacy felt impossible as my toddlers demanded constant attention, even following me into the bathroom. Some living situations or circumstances make privacy difficult on a personal level, like incarceration, a controlling relationship, or close living quarters.

Creating Privacy

Consider for a moment the ways that privacy (whether safeguards or limitations) shows up in your life. Review the examples below and think about other ways to ensure more privacy in our modern world.

- Security systems for the home or vehicle
- Changing passwords and authentication methods
- Encryption with technology
- Deactivating social media or setting accounts to private
- HIPAA policies like releases of information for health information sharing
- Background searches

In our highly connected and virtual world, social media and online presence become other important considerations related to privacy. While I love connecting with new people and keeping up with family and friends, I find myself feeling drained at times and compelled at other times to check statuses. I have learned to check in with myself more to understand why I might feel the need to post some of the things I do. This self-awareness has helped me to curb some unhealthy use of social media.

Privacy Check-In

Taking time to reflect on how privacy shows up in our highly-connected virtual lives helps us to understand how we share information, exchange energy, and show up in the world. Read each statement below and think about whether it strongly, slightly, or doesn't resonate with you and your privacy habits and feelings. After considering each statement, answer the following questions: What stands out to me about privacy after reflecting on these statements? What changes do I want to make in relation to privacy in my life?

- I am comfortable posting pictures of myself on social media.
- I am an open book with others.
- I keep my settings private on social media and only have followers I know.
- I share details about my personal life with only a select few in my inner circle.
- I have no problem sharing my political affiliations or faith practices with others.
- I do not like to tell people when I am traveling.
- I prefer to live in a space that affords privacy with a fence or land.
- My job requires a level of privacy and boundaries.
- I am comfortable sharing my health status with others (weight, illness, etc.)

My Privacy Circle of Comfort

If you have social media, whether for business or social reasons, consider for a moment what you think about before you post something to it. If you aren't on social media, consider what you share with your acquaintances, friends, and closest inner circle.

Fill in the diagram below with things you are comfortable sharing in public (A), on social media (B), with your inner circle (C), and with yourself or a partner only (D).

A. The public world

....

....

....

B. Social media/acquaintances

....

....

....

C. My inner circle

....

....

....

D. Myself

....

....

....

WEEK

6

Harmony at Home

Looking at a plain wall is akin to staring blankly into space. We have a fundamental need for visual nourishment and stimulation in our homes, for our eyes to dance lightly over surfaces and not find them wanting.

— MICHELLE OGUNDEHIN, *Happy Inside*

Our environment plays an important role in our emotional well-being. From colors to space to the flow of energy, our surroundings can influence our mood and behaviors. They offer a chance to reveal our personal style, influence the energy around us, or allow for functionality.

A cluttered space for some might create feelings of anxiety. A lack of organization could contribute to poor time management and stress, resulting in angry outbursts. Lighting is often critical in setting the ambiance and mood for a room — compare natural or soft light to the harshness and intensity of fluorescent lights. Our customized environments can truly reflect our personality.

You may have heard about feng shui, an Asian philosophy and practice of arranging living spaces to reflect the natural world. From an ancient poem connecting human life with the external environment, the Chinese words *feng* and *shui* mean wind and water.[1] In Tao, a philosophy meaning the natural way, feng shui includes key principles like balance and harmony, energy flow, and incorporating the five elements in our surroundings. Even if you choose not to follow feng shui closely, its principles and ideals make sense in creating a nurturing and balanced environment for living.

In practicing feng shui, the command position is the main position or place for a person in each room, such as the bed in a bedroom, a desk in an office, or the stove in a kitchen. These placements should allow you to see the door without being in direct line of the door, giving a sense of command. Another consideration with feng shui involves the flow of energy or *qi* throughout the space. Too much clutter or lack of space inhibits energy flow, which is vital to nurturing life-giving forces. If *qi* becomes blocked, it creates obstacles and stagnation.

In feng shui, with its roots in Taoism, the five elements of fire, earth, metal, water, and wood represent the energy found in the natural world. Each element holds certain properties and meanings, and different materials or colors reflect them in the surroundings. See the below exercise for more detail.

Consider also the colors you choose in your home. While not exhaustively empirically studied, it is evident that

Feng Shui It

Think about some décor ideas for including the following elements in your home.

FIRE:
inspiration and clarity
(red, fire and light, triangles)

EARTH:
groundedness and stability
(earth tones or yellow and tan, tile/stone/pottery, squares)

METAL:
beauty and detail
(white or metallics, metal, circles)

WATER:
intuition and emotion
(black or dark blue, water/mirrors, abstract shapes)

WOOD:
growth and healing
(green or teal, plants/trees/wood, columns)

color impacts our thoughts, feelings, behaviors, and even body responses. Our moods often change based on the colors around us, and companies invest in color research to influence consumer behaviors.

While somewhat collective across humanity, as the limited research shows, color preferences can also have roots in cultural and religious associations.

White, for example, in our Western world, seems to represent innocence and purity, like a bridal gown. In other cultures, white is the color chosen for grief and loss, but black is associated with mourning in the Western world. Cultural implications and spiritual beliefs also use color for different meanings, as evidenced by the chakras system, crystals and stones, religious ceremonies, and celebrations.[2]

Color Associations

RED
Passion, energy, excitement, action, strength

ORANGE
Pleasure, youth, optimism, freedom

YELLOW
Joy, positivity, fun, curiosity, happiness

GREEN
Nature, growth, prosperity, loyalty, luck

BLUE
Loyalty, trust, success, calm, confidence

PURPLE
Fantasy, imagination, royalty, spirituality, justice

PINK
Femininity, softness, respect, creativity, calm, gratitude[3]

Your Dream Space

Imagine what your ideal dream living space might look like. What colors, shapes, and materials would you include? Consider incorporating feng shui or color meaning into your space. Draw or describe your dream room or space in the area below.

Safety in Relationships

*As you remove toxic people from your life,
you free up space and emotional energy for positive,
healthy relationships.*

— JOHN MARK GREEN

Think about times you might have been wounded or hurt by others or situations during your life. Humans have an amazing capacity to rely on mental defenses to protect themselves from feeling hurt, rejected, or abandoned. While defenses help with survival, our brains do not differentiate between a real or a perceived threat. This allows potential distortions in our perceptions to cloud reality and activate unnecessary, even counterproductive defenses.

As a therapist, I explain that we have defense mechanisms to protect us from trauma or hurt. It's an adaptive quality and, at times, truly an amazing feature of our brains. Over time, though, defense mechanisms can become maladaptive and cause issues in our relationships and functioning. Defense mechanisms fall along a spectrum of primitive to more evolved defenses depending on developmental stages. By adulthood, more mature defenses exist to draw upon during times of distress.

Let's take a closer look at the different kinds of defenses and how they show up in our lives. There are different levels of defense mechanisms that range from pathological to immature, neurotic, and mature. Pathological, immature, and neurotic defense mechanisms are more primitive in nature and tend to develop in childhood. Mature defense mechanisms tend to be less primitive and more adaptive in nature. As you read through these defenses, think of how each one might show up in your life.

Pathological

Denial: Refusing to accept or believe reality or fact to protect from a painful situation.

Example: An alcoholic does not believe they have a problem, despite negative consequences from their drinking.

Delusional projection: Delusions, often persecutory in nature, like those found in psychotic disorders.

Example: Someone believes that anyone wearing sunglasses is out to kill them. (This is a true story from my experience.)

Immature

Projection: Putting your uncomfortable or unacceptable thoughts, feelings, or behaviors onto another person as if they are theirs. Comes from a lack of insight or acknowledgment of feelings.

Example: You tell someone that they are angry and being mean when you are actually the one doing this.

Passive aggression: Indirectly expressing hostility covertly.

Example: Getting back at the boss by not completing an assignment in time when you felt the deadline was unfair.

Acting out: Engaging in behaviors to show thoughts or feelings that one cannot share verbally. Can sometimes relieve pressure or built-up emotions, like in a child's temper tantrum.

Example: Punching a hole in the wall rather than using words to express your feelings.

Regression: Reverting to an earlier developmental stage when upset or feeling uncomfortable emotions.

Example: A thirteen-year-old becomes clingy and wets the bed after experiencing a traumatic event.

Neurotic

Rationalization: Changing the meaning or reasoning for thinking, feeling, or doing something to give permission to oneself for the situation.

Example: Someone justifies that it is okay to speed because they believe the speed limit is too slow and no cops are around.

Reaction formation: Changing uncomfortable thoughts or feelings into the exact opposite and often to the extreme.

Example: A server has angry feelings toward a difficult and demanding patron but becomes overly polite and accommodating.

Dissociation: Losing track of time and self-awareness to cope with the present uncomfortable situation by creating a new sense of self. Often found in those having extreme trauma or child abuse. This can develop into a full dissociative identity disorder in extreme cases. Compartmentalizing is a milder form of dissociation.

Example: A mild form of dissociation might be someone imagining they are somewhere else, like the beach, while having a dental procedure.

Displacement: Putting thoughts, feelings, and urges toward one person or situation onto another unrelated person or situation. Used when unable to safely express feelings toward another person, though it causes harm and confusion to the person receiving the displacement.

Example: Getting yelled at by a teacher and then being mean to a younger sibling.

Repression: Blocking uncomfortable thoughts, feelings, and urges through unconsciously pushing down events or situations out of awareness.

Example: Unconsciously pushing down the memory of an abusive event as a child and having no recollection of anything happening.

Suppression: The conscious pushing away of uncomfortable thoughts, feelings, or urges, often using distraction or other methods.

Example: Consciously choosing to not think about something upsetting by distracting yourself with a book or movie.

Mature

Intellectualizing: Using logic and rational thoughts to understand a situation that causes uncomfortable feelings or urges.

Example: Learning your mom has cancer and researching all about the illness and treatment options.

Sublimation and humor: Refocusing uncomfortable or unwanted thoughts, feelings, and impulses into more of a socially acceptable or appropriate manner.

Example: Channeling rage and anger into exercise; using humor to deflect and lighten the mood.

Compensation: Focusing on a strength to make up for a lack of something to help reinforce self-worth. In the extreme, this becomes less evolved and turns into overcompensation, ignoring all flaws or imperfections with an over-focus on the strength to a self-absorbed level.

Example: When not doing well in chess, someone focuses on their ability to excel at word games.

Altruism: Helping and serving others to redirect unwanted and uncomfortable feelings.

Example: Volunteering at a local school when grieving the loss of a child.

Assertiveness: Clear and concise expression of wants and needs firmly and directly.

Example: Asking for your food to be fixed when the order comes out undercooked.

Another important consideration in nurturing safety in relationships involves boundaries. What exactly does it mean to set a boundary? Boundaries, starting where one person ends and another begins, allow for the protection of energy and space.

In the past, I thought about boundaries as something a person puts up to protect themselves from others. Upon further study and understanding, I have learned that boundaries also include the way we show up in another person's life. Sometimes we cross boundaries when we take responsibility for others' feelings, which looks like people-pleasing. Other times, boundaries keep others from hurting us.

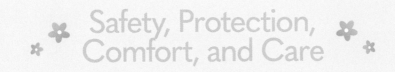

Safety, Protection, Comfort, and Care

What things help you feel safe and protected? Consider physical, emotional, and spiritual safety.

....

....

What steps do you take to create safety for your physical being?

....

....

How do you ensure your emotional safety? What qualities do you look for in a safe person (for example: validating, honest, gentle)?

....

....

What do you do for spiritual protection (for example: prayer, superstition, cleanse, crystals, bubbles)?

....

....

My Relationships

Think about a relationship you currently have. It could be with a partner, parent, sibling, friend, coworker, supervisor, or teacher. Consider ways that defense mechanisms show up in this dynamic. Answer some of the questions below to examine more about your relationship.

My relationship with: ....

....

....

Defense mechanisms present: ....

....

....

Can I share my true thoughts and feelings without
creating conflict or a problem? ....

....

....

How does or doesn't this person validate my ideas,
thoughts, and feelings? ....

....

....

Does this person call me names or make me feel unworthy
in any way? Do I engage in name-calling? ....

....

....

When do I find myself not openly sharing with this person?

....

....

....

Does manipulation show up as a dynamic in this relationship?
(Manipulation involves wanting someone to feel something
so you can gain something.)

....

....

....

Does anyone in the relationship shut down like a stone wall
or give the silent treatment?

....

....

....

Am I free and comfortable to be my authentic self when
I'm around this person?

....

....

....

How do I find myself pretending or exaggerating to chase or impress
this person?

....

....

....

· WEEK ·

8

Sleep in Tired Bodies

*I love the silent hour of night, for blissful dreams
may then arise, revealing to my charmed sight,
what may not bless my waking eyes!*

— ANNE BRONTË, "Night"

While much of this workbook reflects on the emotional aspects of nurturing, sleep is an important physiological component to consider. Restorative sleep, an essential function, allows our bodies to recover and repair themselves from the day before. When disrupted, a lack of sleep can show up in irritability and mood changes, lack of concentration and focus, reduced immunity, and daytime fatigue. Nurturing quality sleep becomes critical for optimal brain functioning and health.

Many factors might contribute to disruptions in our sleep cycles, from insomnia, aging, and circadian rhythm dysfunction to caffeinated beverages. Effective sleep hygiene involves developing habits and creating an environment conducive to ensure a good night of shut-eye. Humans have an internal clock, called our circadian rhythm, that drives our feelings of tiredness and alertness, prompting sleep at night and awakening in the morning. Optimal cell functioning and regulation depend on our circadian rhythm.

Consider how traveling to different time zones creates jet lag or how changes in daylight savings impact energy levels. As we age, our circadian rhythm becomes more worn and sometimes impaired, affecting our quality and quantity of sleep. Nurturing our bodies and practicing good sleep hygiene can help reshape our natural circadian rhythm functioning.

One of the worst feelings in the world involves being tired and unable to fall asleep. Insomnia wreaks havoc on lives and causes bigger issues in functioning and our health. It can take the form of difficulty falling asleep, waking up throughout the night, or early morning awakening with an inability to fall back asleep.

Understanding brain chemistry helps us understand insomnia. In the simplest explanation, serotonin, a neurotransmitter in the brain, helps make the hormone melatonin. Melatonin signals sleepiness when it becomes dark outside. Making improvements in day and nighttime routines, like setting regular hours for sleep or increasing exercise during the day, as well as trying natural supplements or medications to aid

A Sleep Hygiene Lullaby

Here are some steps you can take to prioritize sleep and follow a good sleep hygiene practice. Feel free to personalize your own formula.

- Lighting (dim and yellow to help activate melatonin)
- Warm bath
- Relaxation techniques like meditation, deep breathing, or progressive muscle relaxation
- Warm tea
- Comfy bedding or clothing
- Cooler temperatures (about 65°F/18°C)
- Stretching/yoga
- White noise machine
- Engaging in physical activity during the day/afternoon (not immediately before bedtime)
- Limiting phone, computer, or television screens
- Limiting naps
- Fixed wake and sleep times
- Limiting caffeine, alcohol, and nicotine
- Using your bed only for sleep

with sleep, can prove helpful. It is crucial to nurture restorative sleep for our mental, physical, and emotional well-being, no matter the method.

A full sleep cycle involves completion through five stages, including rapid eye movement or REM stage, where dreaming takes place. The brain repairs itself during these stages of wakefulness and deeper sleep. Completing sleep cycles is quite important, because waking up in the middle of one stage of sleep can cause drowsiness.

Dreaming is actually an important function for repairing the brain and takes place during the REM stage, the most important stage of deep sleep. REM allows for information collected throughout the day, including emotions or memories, to become fully processed. The lack of visual

stimulation during sleep keeps some chemicals from activating as normal, allowing strong emotions or traumas to reprocess in a calmer and less triggering environment. This reprocessing and repair that happens during REM allows for more efficiency and brain functioning in general.

Fascinatingly, awakening during REM allows us to recall dreams. We might not recall dreaming if we wake up at the end of REM or during another sleep phase. Sometimes, dreams can offer clues to strong emotional conflicts or traumas that need reprocessing. While some dreams might include extraneous, unimportant details, other themes and feelings that emerge can clue us into recognizing suppressed emotions that we might distract ourselves from when awake.

Dream Journaling

While there isn't space in this book for a full-blown dream journal,
here is an exercise to get you started in dream journaling. Consider
using a separate notebook to dream journal for a full week.

The night before you sleep, write down what happened that day.
The next day, in the other spaces, describe your dream and how it made
you feel. Make sure you complete these as soon as you wake up, because
dreams are quickly forgotten. In the last space, search the internet for
dream symbols and have some fun recording your interpretation.

Events from the Day

Dream Detail

Emotions

Interpretation

Self-Care for Stressed Minds

*Almost everything will work again if
you unplug it for a few minutes, including you.*
— ANNE LAMOTT

From bubble baths and shower bombs or naps to more costly massages, spa days, and vacations, making time and space for relaxation allows us to nurture our minds and bodies. For some, relaxation is highly individualized, and what might feel soothing or relaxing can differ depending on personal preference, sensitivity, or experiences.

Self-care can involve nurturing our bodies by finding pleasing sensory experiences to indulge in, like a hot bath, a relaxing massage, or wearing a favorite perfume. It also involves rest and boundary-setting, as discussed in previous chapters on prioritizing our time. For some, eating a balanced diet with whole foods or moving our bodies in different ways creates feelings of caring for the body. This sensory aspect is an important consideration to add to an intentional practice. While I love the idea of a spa day or nature hike, life demands don't always allow for this luxury. I propose that relaxation should include larger and perhaps

scheduled activities while simultaneously incorporating daily rituals and routines that promote centering, winding down, reenergizing, or decompressing.

As a therapist seeing clients all day, I found that I needed a break from back-to-back sessions. I have learned to create a sacred space that I do not mess with during my lunch break. I do not answer calls or return emails or messages from anyone during this time. Having quiet both externally and internally allows me to shut off my analytical brain and helps reenergize me for the afternoon. Many people find a similar experience in early morning hours before others wake up while

Taking Stock

For this exercise, first reflect on the *current* ways you nurture relaxation in each of the categories shown below, both on a daily/weekly basis and on a longer-term basis, to get an honest snapshot of what your life looks like. Try to be honest with yourself — don't list things you want to do in theory but don't practice. Honesty allows for filling in gaps and setting bigger intentions.

After reflecting on your current behaviors, think about where relaxation is especially lacking in your life and what new behaviors you may be able to incorporate.

they drink a cup of coffee or sit on the back porch. These little routines and rituals allow for a small and necessary consistent dose of relaxation.

Nurturing necessarily includes the mind, body, and spirit, but I propose also incorporating a fourth component: your surroundings. The external world around us has immense power to become either draining or energizing. For example, consider working in a cubicle all day and finding time during a small break to go outside for a walk and watch the birds.

When I was a child, my family took a relaxing weeklong vacation every summer at the beach. As an adult, I haven't always made time for relaxation due to financial, parenting, or other demands. Driven by worry, I believed taking time off would disappoint others, or that I might not have enough money to pay bills. My kids were twelve and thirteen before we took our first real vacation, outside of visiting family, for a Disney cruise.

It makes me feel a little sad that I haven't always modeled the importance of nurturing relaxation and self-care for my children. Making relaxation and ourselves a priority involves releasing feelings of guilt. We must recognize that self-care allows us to become the best version of ourselves and build a life worth living. Without taking this time to recharge and relax, the mind, body, and soul become depleted, and hearts grow weary and filled with discontent.

It is essential to examine your barriers to making relaxation a priority. Fully understanding barriers allows for finding ways to overcome them and examine faulty beliefs that impede growth. While joyful and inspiring words feel nice, sometimes focusing on the negative blocks proves helpful. What drives that belief or obstacle? What function does it serve? Perhaps to protect or defend against hurt. Perhaps deeper shame-based beliefs from childhood or trauma. Creative problem solving comes from opening to all the possibilities.

Troubleshooting Barriers to Relaxation

How might you overcome these common barriers to relaxation?

- Overthinking
- Too busy
- Perfectionism
- Negative self-talk and beliefs

Relaxation

Think about all the possibilities for relaxation. Check off some of your favorite ways to relax, and feel free to draw and add your own!

☐ Hot bath

☐ Reading

☐ Sunbathing

☐ Music

☐ Nature walk

☐ Crafting

☐ Travel

☐ Exercise

☐ Running

☐ Art

Radical Acceptance in Stubborn Minds

Watch your thoughts, they become your words; watch your words, they become your actions; watch your actions, they become your habits; watch your habits, they become your character; watch your character, it becomes your destiny.

— UNKNOWN

Radical acceptance, a term that comes from practicing mindfulness, allows for being in the moment and fully accepting reality as it exists without judgment, even when it is uncomfortable. Radical acceptance does not mean allowing or agreeing with the discomfort. It involves leaning into pain while suspending meaning and attachment to this pain.

Radical acceptance can feel counterintuitive, particularly when experiencing pain. When distorted, it sounds callous, passive, or invalidating, almost inviting suffering. But radical acceptance does not mean complacency — for you must accept a situation first before making a change.

For example, consider the COVID-19 pandemic. Most would agree that it has deeply impacted lives and caused disruption and inconvenience at the least and tragedy and loss at the most. Radically accepting the pandemic, no matter the perspective, simply

sounds like "the pandemic has caused suffering in our lives." This acceptance acknowledges the harmful as a fact. It does not judge or attempt to change it. By accepting pain, we can move toward focusing energy on what we have control over instead of becoming stuck in misery and suffering.

Most people have a running mindset of evaluating and judging situations, events, people, and things as good or bad, right or wrong, fair or unfair. This constant judgment shifts us away from the moment and creates a new, emotionally charged mindset, one that makes it almost impossible to stay in the present or find a sense of peace.

It is important to note that this does not mean we shouldn't evaluate or judge situations. But acceptance must happen before harmful situations can change. To change something involves not becoming hijacked by a new moment or emotional state; otherwise, focus becomes lost. It feels challenging to accept and allow before change. This statement does not apply to radically accepting and not acting on situations that need changing, like injustice, violence, or hatred. This statement instead helps our internal reality and allows presence in our lives.

Radical acceptance feels uncomfortable. How can we just allow something harmful? I repeat, radical acceptance does not mean inaction. It involves becoming fully aware of and accepting a situation to determine if a change needs to happen — because the constant pursuit of changing something that can't change becomes crazy-making. It reminds me of the serenity prayer[4]: learning the wisdom to know the difference between things we can change and things we can't.

It Is What It Is

Reframe the following statements from good versus bad into more neutral statements. Notice how each statement evokes a different internal experience when removing the judgment. For example, let's reframe this statement: "Cold weather is the worst." How can we change it to state a fact or describe what is happening without saying it is good or bad? How about: "Cold weather makes me shiver and want to stay inside."

The sun is so hot and miserable.

People are annoying.

We have no control over COVID-19.

This is the worst thing that can happen.

I can't stand...

Individuals who haven't mastered radical acceptance yet often seem to make life harder or more complicated for themselves. For example, let's say a teenager in a traditional school doesn't think teachers should give homework on the weekends, and therefore boycotts it. While the teen may have a valid point, the school district and teachers aren't going to change course in that moment of the teen's decision to not do his homework that weekend.

This doesn't mean the kid's perspective is invalid or that he or she shouldn't advocate or act toward changing the policy. At that moment, though, resisting and fighting against doing homework by refusing to complete assignments would simply lead to poor grades. Is this the most effective way to handle the situation? Accepting that this is the reality and that the homework needs to be done allows for more effective choices. Again, the teen doesn't have to like it, agree with it, think it's fair, or feel comfortable with it. It just means he or she must accept that it is the current situation and make an effective decision.

A Story

Here's a simple story to illustrate the concept of radical acceptance.

There once was a woman who had a long-haired Persian cat. She loved her grumpy-faced cat and would hug and cuddle with him. The cat would shed, leaving hair all over the place — the couch, her clothes, and the furniture. She tried to find ways to keep the cat from shedding, like brushing and supplements. She looked at ways to keep the cat off the furniture, yet the cat hair persisted, impossible to stop.

The moral of the story? If you're going to have a long-haired cat, you must learn to accept cat hair.

Continuing to obsess and get upset will keep you stuck in a never-ending cycle. Radical acceptance cuts through this, allowing for more peace of mind and tolerance.

How does this story make you feel? What aspects can you relate to? What does it feel like to try to fix something you can't change?

Yeah, But…

Think about something happening in your life that
sometimes feels difficult to manage or deal with. Let's practice
radical acceptance to help detach from the suffering or struggles.

Describe the situation:

What can you accept?

What can't you accept?

Is this something you can ultimately control?

What feels uncomfortable about letting go of the control?

What would it feel like to accept and allow this situation?

Explore the "yeah, buts" here:

Your Life's Purpose

Believe in your heart that you're meant to live a life full of passion, purpose, magic and miracles.

— ROY T. BENNETT, *The Light in the Heart*

Have you ever sat and wondered about the meaning of life and your purpose for living? Talk about the origins of an existential crisis! Often these ponderings may lead us down a path that stirs up both positive and negative emotions, causing us to realize that we feel unfulfilled, stuck, or lost in our lives. We may find ourselves experiencing a growing discontent from an unfulfilling career or think we do not make a difference in the world.

Discerning our life purpose can prove daunting, particularly in the modern world. Societal conditioning and expectations may conflict with familial, cultural, and religious influences. Sometimes we find ourselves taking a path that differs from our true selves. Finding alignment with our core values, while important, can feel overwhelming and difficult.

The Japanese have a concept called ikigai that means "reason for being." This compound word combines the Japanese word "iki," meaning "life," and "kai," meaning "result, worth, use."[5]

Combined, this creates the powerful concept of making a life worth living. The beauty of ikigai comes from the Eastern world's appreciation of life's simple pleasures and finding meaning in smaller, ordinary moments, rather than exclusively focusing on grandiose concepts like legacy and achievement.

The concept of ikigai reminds me of an elderly man whom I'll call "Mr. Tuck," whom I visited at a nursing home while volunteering with an adopt-a-grandparent program in college. As a busy student, I enjoyed spending a simple hour with Mr. Tuck. Kind and gentle, he accepted each moment of his daily routine, from eating lunch, watching the birds, and talking about his memories of his apple farm and military days to forever trying to set me up with his single grandson.

Mr. Tuck exemplified ikigai. He embraced the joy of being in the moment, reminiscing on his golden memories, and making the best of living in a nursing home. My visits with

Mr. Tuck taught me that perhaps our purpose comes not from external measures of success like money or grandly making a large impact on the world. Perhaps, instead, our purpose comes from finding meaning and beauty in appreciating the simplicity and complexity of life, no matter the circumstances.

In our Western world, we have adapted the idea of "finding our purpose" to a

Which Values Resonate with You?

Take a look at the listed values below. Which values do you tend to resonate with? Remember, these are different perspectives and not right or wrong.

Western Values	Eastern Values
Achievements and success	Self-awareness and development of true self
Future-focused, goal-oriented	Meaning found in the present moment
Independence and self-reliance	United "we"; collective
Equality	Satisfaction with what one has

model you may have seen before called the Purpose Venn Diagram. (This has sometimes been mislabeled as the ikigai model.) This model can be a useful lens through which to analyze our purpose, but it has some faults — namely, that not everyone has the time, health, or ability to develop skills and be paid for them. The model could contribute to feeling lost and purposeless if certain people, such as a person who lives in a nursing home, is a stay-at-home parent, or has a disability, attempt to meet the concepts outlined in it.

The Purpose Venn Diagram[6]

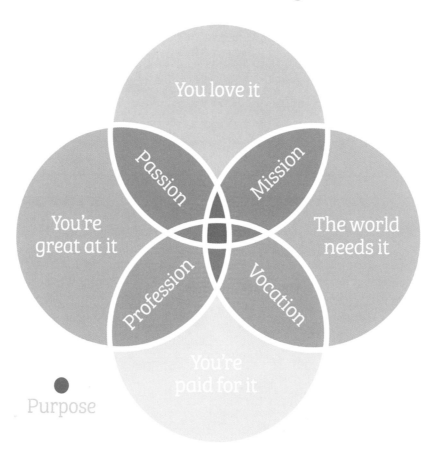

You love it

Passion

Mission

You're great at it

The world needs it

Profession

Vocation

You're paid for it

Purpose

So, while the Purpose model does offer an excellent framework for considering key elements and finding balance and meaning in our lives, I think it is important to consider blending the Eastern and Western perspectives for a more comprehensive and inclusive model. For this reason, I developed my own model, called the Nurturing Life's Purpose model, which reflects both concepts of ikigai and purpose.

Nurturing Life's Purpose Model

Nurturing Ikigai

This exercise helps determine your values and life purpose using both the Purpose Venn Diagram and my Nurturing Life's Purpose model to reflect the concept of ikigai. I have included examples from my own life.

Purpose Venn Diagram

What I Love + What the World Needs = My Mission

Example:
Helping people + Mental health support

....

....

What the World Needs + What I Can Get Paid For = My Vocation

Example:
Mental health support + Becoming a therapist/writing a book

....

....

What I Can Get Paid For + What I Am Good At = My Profession

Example:
Becoming a therapist/writing a book +
Connecting with others, creativity, writing

....

....

What I Am Good At + What I Love = My Passion

Example:
Connecting with others, creativity, writing + Helping people

....

....

Nurturing Your Life's Purpose Model

What I Love and Value +
How I Appreciate the Moment = My Desires

Example:
Authenticity and learning + Tuning into my five senses

....

....

How I Appreciate the Moment + How I Spend My Time = My Zen

Example:
Tuning into my five senses + In nature or analyzing

....

....

How I Spend My Time + My Gifts and Strengths = My Worth

Example:
In nature or analyzing + Creativity and helping others

....

....

My Gifts and Strengths + What I Love and Value = My Purpose

Example:
Creativity and helping others + Authenticity and learning

....

....

Motivation in Stuck Brains

Be brave enough to live the life of your dreams according to your vision and purpose instead of the expectations and opinions of others.

— ROY T. BENNETT, *The Light in the Heart*

Procrastination. For some, that word might evoke uncomfortable, stressful feelings. For others, it might create a feeling of temporary relief in putting something off for later. And for some, it might even help them step into high gear, coming down to the last minute.

Life can often become a balancing act between the have-tos and the want-tos. When consumed with doing too much, motivation can come to a screeching halt. Other times, motivation can hide behind fear of failure or avoidance of uncomfortable feelings. Getting started becomes half the battle, and knowing our de-motivators can help us develop an action plan.

Newton's first law of motion comes to mind. An object at rest stays at rest, while an object in motion stays in motion with the same speed and direction unless an unbalanced force causes it to change. So, while I sit on my couch procrastinating, it's going to take some other force to get me up and moving. In fact, a creative and exciting video call with my awesome publisher and design team helped motivate me to complete this chapter!

Experts agree that when struggling with motivation, the most important step involves taking some form of action, even if just for five to ten minutes. Usually, momentum picks up once the going gets started. Knowing your work habits helps, as some people might work best with built-in breaks or partializing larger tasks into smaller steps. I prefer to do an all-or-nothing thing myself. Either way, the key is just getting started!

Consider the following illustration. Perhaps you have put off doing the dishes in the sink because the dishwasher, full of clean dishes, needs unloading first. The task of washing or rinsing dishes seems even more overwhelming, thinking about having to first unload the dishwasher. Using the Newtonian law of motion, see what happens once you get started. Start with saying, "I will just unload the cups." I just tried it and ended up unloading the whole dishwasher. Then I couldn't stop there. I ended up loading the dishwasher with dirty dishes and even washing some pans and pots! Such a simple task that feels daunting when procrastinating becomes doable once in action.

This concept works when suffering from depression or anxiety as well. Often small, simple tasks like doing laundry, bathing, or even getting mail become overwhelming and feel impossible. Breaking the activity into smaller tasks allows for a small win and a step in the right direction.

Perhaps your lack of motivation stems from feeling uninspired or stuck. Perhaps you struggle with depression, grief, or even exhaustion. Many factors can contribute to a lack of motivation, from burnout to physical or mental struggles. Understanding your de-motivators and what fuels your procrastination is an important step in problem-solving.

An Object in Motion Stays in Motion

Let's try a physics experiment. Think about something you don't feel like doing and have been procrastinating. Now, set a timer for five minutes and get started on the first step of that task.

What happened once you got started for five minutes? How did you feel? Hey, at the very least, you logged five minutes toward your task!

Some common reasons for procrastinating involve fear of making a mistake or failure; waiting for motivation, energy, or inspiration; feeling overwhelmed and exhausted already; or even wanting to do more fun or easier things first. I call this exhausted and depleted aspect the Giving Tree Syndrome. In the children's book *The Giving Tree,* Shel Silverstein shares a story about a tree that lovingly gave its leaves, branches, and trunk over time to a young boy who grew into an old man. At the end of the book, the kind giving tree, now only a stump, still offered the old man a place to sit.

Sometimes giving and giving without replenishing or nurturing contributes to procrastination because exhaustion emerges. You can't give if you've got nothing left. Finding ways to create balance by filling up our cups allows us to stay motivated and focused on important things. For givers and those kindhearted people, it allows us to keep giving!

Here are some questions for reflection.

- What keeps you blocked?
- Are you avoiding something? If so, what?
- What feelings come up for you?

The Giving Tree Syndrome

What are ways you give and sacrifice parts of yourself and your time to others? What are ways you replenish yourself by nurturing or accepting help? Are you achieving balance between the two?

Giving to Others

Nurturing Myself

Let's Get Motivated!

To get motivated with a big task, break it down into smaller steps and focus on completing one at a time. In this exercise, try planning out a big task this way. I have filled in an example for you.

Goal: **Steps:** **Outcome:**

Writing book

- Write outline and chapter headings
- Start introduction
- Come up with main activities
- Come up with basic ideas and smaller activities

- Write basic narrative
- Edit and write better
- Resources, citation, and quotes

Complete manuscript by deadline

Visualization for Future Minds

Live your vision and demand your success.

— STEVE MARABOLI, *Life, the Truth, and Being Free*

Bidding farewell to winter and greeting the eagerly anticipated spring calls for reflection on your vision for the upcoming seasons. With crocuses blooming through the snow after a winter hopefully filled with rest and restoration, the winter to spring transition offers a wonderful time for nurturing a vision of our coming year.

One of my favorite activities for the New Year's holiday involves creating a vision board with my family. Getting stickers, craft and scrapbooking supplies, and magazine pictures, we sit around cutting and pasting our vision for the coming year. It seems that simply setting the intention for the coming year helps manifest this vision to fruition. This conscious reflection allows the subconscious mind to find motivation and direction behind the scenes when becoming saturated in the daily pursuits of life.

How often you see your vision board depends on your personal preferences, space, and privacy. I usually prefer to look at my vision board a few times throughout the year when the seasons change to remind myself of my dreams. This allows me not to obsess or become hard on myself if I'm not meeting my goal, while providing an opportunity to remind myself of my vision or adjust as needed. But perhaps you don't want someone to know something you want to work on. Or perhaps you want to share with your tribe for accountability or support. No matter your preferences, a vision board is meant for you!

Of course, some things might manifest in your life without any awareness they're coming. I never envisioned or planned on writing my first book, nor did any of us anticipate a pandemic. The book-writing opportunity just presented itself and created many openings for me to expand in ways I could never imagine. Life has a funny way of working like that. So, while I believe setting intentions and nurturing our dreams is important in accomplishing goals, remember that life sometimes takes us by surprise and forces us outside of our comfort and controlled zones.

You might wonder where to start in making a vision board. What exactly goes into this endeavor? It might sound intimidating or even make you feel vulnerable. The best and first place to start involves simply reflecting on your current situation. Consider what in your present life brings contentment or fulfillment. Think about what things you

Supplies List

While I prefer to create a hands-on vision board using physical craft supplies, others might prefer something more virtual. Regardless of your preference, write out a list of supplies needed for making your vision board.

MY LIST:
Posterboard, magazines, online pictures or images, scissors, glue, stickers, scrapbook stuff

YOUR LIST:

....

....

....

....

....

....

....

might want to change or improve upon. Reflect on experiences, relationships, and values that hold importance in your life.

Here are some helpful questions to consider for imagining your future seasons.

- Who do you want to be surrounded by, and what do you want to be doing?
- What keeps you motivated?
- Who believes in you?
- In what ways does your life reflect your values? What pulls you away from this? What could change to bring you closer to your values?
- What healthier habits or activities do you want to participate in or develop?
- What inspires you to create a life worth living?
- How do you want to fill your time?
- Have you done anything exciting or fun recently?
- What things would you want to do before you die? What keeps you from doing this?
- What steps can you take to move toward a bucket list item or something you've always wanted to do, even if a small step?

If you're like most people, you might have some "yeah, buts" floating around in your mind. When creating something artistic or inspiring, our brains often develop blocks or barriers. This might come from feeling vulnerable or having a more practical mindset about envisioning the future. I can assure you that nothing happens if we don't first consider it a possibility. Furthermore, envisioning blocks and barriers ahead of time allows us to challenge them appropriately or develop a new game plan to help us stay focused on our goal. As a sports mom, I often tell my children to visualize themselves not just making great plays but also making a mistake or screwing up and picturing how they will recover, correct mistakes, and stay focused on the game.

Let's take a closer look at five reasons you might not want to create a vision board. I've included a challenge to consider for each of these "yeah, buts."

1. **It's a waste of time, and you could be more productive doing something else.** Creating a vision board allows us to become more productive when we focus on our desires and goals.

2. **It's stupid and cheesy.** Perhaps making a vision board seems childish. However, creativity often happens when we release those feelings of vulnerability and access a different part of our brain.

3. **What's the point?** Often, setting New Year's resolutions creates a goal with an external measure of failure or accomplishment. Vision boards don't focus on this as much as

incorporating a life worth living and taking stock of ways to improve the quality of life to align with values. The vision board should not be a have-to reminder checklist.

4. **I don't have supplies, time, or money to shop for them.** If you cannot create a physical board, consider doing a virtual board through Pinterest, Gratitude (which has a virtual board option), or *www.udreamr.com*.

5. **I don't have anyone to do it with, or I don't want to share with anyone.** You don't have to share with anyone, or you can share with your support system tribe. This personal exercise sometimes becomes more powerful when shared, but it doesn't have to be. It's designed for you.

Nurturing a vision for the coming seasons creates intention, purpose, and clarity on where and how to focus our energy and attention. It provides a road map and a guide for speaking ideas into existence.

❀ Challenge List ❀

List the challenges to your "yeah, buts" here.

....

....

....

....

....

....

....

....

....

My Vision Board

Use this space to create a miniature vision board, or brainstorm ideas for a vision board that you'll create somewhere else. What things do you want to include? What are some of your values that you want to include? What colors are you drawn to?

Creativity in Practical Minds

*Vulnerability is the birthplace
of innovation, creativity, and change.*

— BRENÉ BROWN

Creativity. Sounds intimidating. I used to think creativity equaled artistic. However, creativity involves the ability to create something new and original using our imagination — and this transcends artwork.

When sitting down to imagine, contemplate, or create something new, it can feel scary and intimidating. Thoughts of self-doubt or fear of failure might rise to the surface. What if it looks stupid, or others think it's dumb? What if this doesn't work? What if I'm not good enough? This mindset seems to develop fully by grade school, when we often learn to compare ourselves to others and get graded on the outcome.

As a play therapist, one of the most important aspects of working with a child involves reflecting on the process and not the outcome. This might sound like commenting on a child's drawing by saying, "Oh wow, what made you choose that color?" or "I love how you are taking your time" rather than "That's great" or "Good job," which focuses on the external result.

When nurturing creativity, learning to suspend judgment and fear allows for all possibilities to come to the surface and the process to become more important than the outcome. Imagine a child, free to create and paint without worries of making a mess, doing it correctly, or having expectations of the outcome. The creative process becomes magical, expanding into endless possibilities.

Overthinking can create a huge disconnect and barrier, as can judgment and fear. Even when unrelated to the creative project, stress and worry limit thinking outside the box and developing innovative solutions to problems.

As a newbie to writing books, when faced with writer's block, taking breaks to recharge in nature helped renew my spirit and made me feel connected with something larger, allowing for greater inspiration. I also found researching and reading topics of interest to whet my appetite inspired ideas. Even music and smells have the power to inspire creativity, as I typically have music playing and candles burning in the background when I write.

Your Inspiration

What inspires you when you feel blocked?
Perhaps nature, your kids, animals, music, your family,
or spiritual practices?

Think about the first time you can remember receiving feedback that crushed your creative spirit. Perhaps an adult giving feedback on using the proper method for coloring or completing schoolwork. Perhaps a parent or coach giving negative feedback, even if the intent came from trying to motivate. Negativity has a way of crushing creativity into smithereens. A growth mindset allows for new ideas and ingenious innovations to spring forth.

While creativity seems connected to the arts, it doesn't have to stop there. In a conversation with my musically talented and certified public accountant (CPA) sister, I asked if she felt bored and unfulfilled at her corporate job, given her talents and creativity. She shocked me by saying that she found ways to use her creativity in her finance job by solving problems and challenges with an out-of-the-box perspective, even in finance. You don't have to be an artist to incorporate creativity into your life.

Dos and Don'ts for Creativity

What do you find helpful for nurturing creativity, and what tends to stifle your creativity? Fill in some more examples.

Do	Don't
Brain dump	Judge
Make mistakes	Strive for perfection
Get comfy	Stay rigid and strict
Evolve and change	Stagnate and do it like always

Spiderweb Mind Map

Think about a specific way that you want to nurture creativity or something you'd like to have in your life; write this in the center. Brainstorm the benefits and positives about the thing you are nurturing or seeking in the outer circles. For each spider, write negative thoughts that might creep in. For example, I want to move to the mountains (center); I might have the outer circles as serenity, healing, hiking, cold weather, and fall leaves, and the spiders as the cost of moving, adjusting to a new state, and having to change my license.

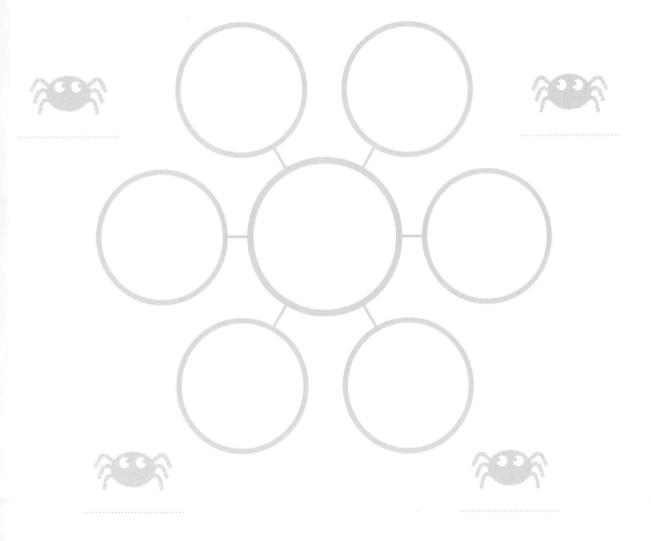

WEEK
15

Dreams in Sheltered Souls

"Don't you find it odd," she continued,
"that when you're a kid, everyone, all the world,
encourages you to follow your dreams. But when you're older,
somehow, they act offended if you even try."
— ETHAN HAWKE, *The Hottest State*

Think for a moment of a dream you had or currently have in your life. Perhaps it's a place to live or a dream job. Having a vision of our future or something that we want allows us to focus our energy on manifesting and turning our dreams into reality.

Without dreams, life becomes meaningless and filled with tasks that have no purpose. Without dreams, we have no direction. Dreams point us on the right path of our heart's content. Dreams don't stagnate or die; they evolve just as we do. Dreams represent the bigger aspects of what we yearn for in life. Not necessarily realistic, our dreams might seem farfetched and impossible, yet dreaming big allows for something to work toward. If you shoot for a big dream, you might end up with a piece of it, or perhaps something even better.

To me, dreams differ from manifestation and vision boards, which is why I included this as a separate chapter. With dreaming, nothing is impossible. Even the most unrealistic dreams have a place in our minds. While nurturing a dream, it becomes important to positively think of all the possibilities. Often, negative thoughts creep in, making a negative outcome more likely. Without positivity, dreams rarely ever happen. Making a dream come true involves the belief that something can happen, which helps propel action toward the future goal.

Nothing seems sadder to me than someone who has given up on their dreams. Even if the dream changes course or evolves, that differs from giving up. Giving up means abandoning and parting ways with something due to fear, negativity, and dejection. While the likelihood of becoming a famous musician might seem slim given the number of people chasing that dream, moving toward a dream is where the magic happens. When aligning with positivity, dreams can morph and evolve and make way for new dreams to blossom. But giving up on a dream ensures that dream will not come true.

As a child, I dreamed of becoming the next Mary Lou Retton, a gold-medal Olympic athlete. Over many years, three-hour practices several times a week and all-day practices with meets on the weekends became a drudgery to me. While I didn't want to disappoint my parents, I made the difficult decision in middle school to quit gymnastics. Even though I had natural talent and dedication, eventually, my dream lost

steam and passion. The decision to quit gymnastics changed my life in many ways and contributed to my becoming a therapist. Dreams can evolve, and we can let go of them. Letting go of a dream due to fear of failure or a negative belief of impossibility can lead to regret. But this differs from releasing a dream that no longer resonates or inspires due to the natural evolution of life.

Have you ever had someone crush your dreams? Maybe they laughed at you. Maybe they told you to get your head out of the clouds or that it would never happen. I can assure you that your dream never happened if you internalized this belief. Many famous and successful people continued to pursue their dreams despite rejection or criticism. For example, rejected thirty times, Stephen King's book *Carrie* was eventually published. And Michael Jordan, cut from his high school basketball team, went on to play at UNC Chapel Hill and become one of the greatest basketball players.

The Evolving Dream

Think about a dream you had as a small child. What happened to this dream? Who supported and encouraged you? How did they show their support? How did this dream change, become a reality, or disappear? What would you tell your younger self about this dream?

Pay attention to the motives or intent of internal and external critics. Perhaps the critical voice, whether yours or a loved one's, wants to protect you from disappointment, hurt, or rejection. Or perhaps a critical person feels envious or has an ulterior motive toward you not reaching your dreams that has nothing to do with your ability. It's worth further exploration and contemplation.

Learning to silence our inner or outer critics helps make dreams reality. While the likelihood of a dream coming true might depend on factors like talent, timing, and resources, dreams always have the potential to evolve into something amazing. Consider someone who dreams of being a famous musician but doesn't have the best voice or instrumental skills. Perhaps they develop their songwriting skills or work in the music industry. Wouldn't life be so boring if we believed our inner and outer critics?

Dream Buster versus Dream Maker

A positive and growth mindset allows for steps toward following our dreams and opening doors to all the possibilities. What holds you back from your dreams?

Dream Busters	Dream Makers
I'm not good enough.	I am learning to accept my gifts and strengths.
It will never happen.	It won't happen if I never try.
It's too farfetched.	Many things once seemed farfetched, like electricity, home computers, and smartphones.
No one believes I can do it.	Just because others don't believe I can doesn't mean I need to agree or that it's the truth.

Dare to Dream

In this exercise, let's take some time to explore our dreams.
Fill in the space below with details about your dreams. Feel free to
think big here with all the possibilities. Instead of shooting down ideas
or focusing on the impossible, dream big with no limitations!

Change in Static Lives

Similar to a butterfly, I've gone through a metamorphosis, been released from my dark cocoon, embraced my wings, and soared!

— DANA ARCURI, *Reinventing You!: Simple Steps to Transform Your Body, Mind & Spirit*

With springtime in the air, nothing more beautifully illustrates change and metamorphosis than the miracle of a caterpillar's transformation into a butterfly. I used to think caterpillars rested during the chrysalis stage, safely tucked away and waiting for butterfly magic to happen.

But what happens inside the chrysalis isn't relaxing at all. The caterpillar's digestive fluids completely break down its body tissue on a cellular level, dissolving the caterpillar into a group of undifferentiated cells. These imaginal cells form new parts like wings, antennae, eyes, and legs — a whole new body.[7] Once fully developed, the butterfly can make its great escape into the world a transformed creature.

As humans, we yearn for security and safety. Yet all creatures, like the butterfly, must learn to adapt and allow change for survival and evolution — even when that process feels like dissolving into a hot, gooey mess. While painful and messy, change brings about something amazing and beautiful, and the journey becomes a celebration.

While the human cycle of change doesn't usually involve bodies dissolving, people can go through ego deaths and evolve in learning and growth. Letting go of unnecessary self-protection behaviors or mindsets against pain and suffering allows growth and evolution. Although developed for treating addictions, the addiction model of change explains how humans might go about making any kind of change in their lives. Here are its five stages.

1. **Precontemplation:** Denial that a problem that needs to change even exists
2. **Contemplation:** Recognizing the problem but not wanting to act or do anything
3. **Action:** Developing and modifying a plan and steps to make changes toward a goal
4. **Maintenance:** Continuing the action path
5. **Relapse:** Reverting to life before the changes

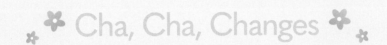

Cha, Cha, Changes

Fill in each stage to better understand how this model of change applies to your life. Think about a situation you want or are currently in the process of changing.

Precontemplation. How are you aware of the problem?

....

....

Contemplation. Why do you want to change? Why have you not taken action?

....

....

Action. What steps can you take to change?

....

....

Maintenance. How can you continue to stay on track?

....

....

Relapse. What can you do to prevent reverting to old patterns?

....

....

This model recognizes potential resistance to change. For example, in the precontemplation stage, it would become premature to discuss action steps. The person hasn't recognized the importance of changing or isn't fully committed. Focusing on the reasons why change makes sense becomes the first step. Once a person is in the contemplation stage, they might still have barriers to taking actual steps toward the change. Finding solutions to overcome those barriers or reinforcing the reason for wanting to change can help propel someone into the action phase.

When presented with something that rocks our world, a crisis can devolve into disaster, creating grief, loss, trauma, and hardships. Yet it also creates an opportunity for evolution, growth, new beginnings, learning, and wisdom, albeit sometimes painfully. Think about your life so far and how you have changed through the years. Look at the times when significant changes and metamorphoses happened in your life through what felt like a crisis.

In these moments, something big shifts, propelling us into chaos and strong emotions while presenting an opportunity for healing, growth, and forward movement. Career changes, divorce, new relationships, relocation, or losing a family member or friend evoke feelings of stress and anxiety, reflecting that change can feel scary and overwhelming.

The insurance and health industries offer a helpful assessment tool to determine the ranking of stressful life events. I find these assessments validating, as change can feel overwhelming when dealing with multiple major life events. The Holmes-Rahe Stress Inventory (1967) and the Perceived Stress Scale (1994) provide validated and helpful measurements of how stressful our lives are and how our perception of stress impacts our lives.[8]

My Metamorphosis

What are you afraid of changing in your world? Kids going off to college, ending a relationship, changing jobs, relocating? Complete the following inventory of changes and ways they might feel scary to you.

Describe a change or something that needs to change in your life:

What stage do you find yourself in: caterpillar, cocooning and dissolving, or butterfly?

What are you afraid of?

What are your barriers or excuses?

What would life look like after the change?

What support do you need?

What needs to happen?

Courage in Vulnerable Hearts

Courage is the most important of all the virtues. Because without courage, you can't practice any other virtue consistently. You can be kind and true and fair and generous and just, and even merciful, occasionally, but to be that thing time after time, you have to really have courage.

— MAYA ANGELOU

Nurturing courage to make changes or take risks necessary for growth must involve understanding fear and our body's stress response. Fear, an important emotion, causes us to react toward a real or perceived threat to ensure our well-being and safety. This emotion can trigger the fight, flight, freeze, or fawn stress response in our bodies. When triggered, our sympathetic nervous system allows for a surge of chemical and hormonal responses in our bodies that helps protect us from danger by fighting off a threat or fleeing to safety.

Our primitive ancestors detected these signals through their senses. In our modern day and age, with fewer consistent threats to our physical safety, this fight-or-flight mechanism can result from perceived stressors and threats as well as emotions. For instance, driving in rush-hour traffic might prove stressful, even triggering a fight-or-flight reaction in our bodies, yet traffic typically is not life-threatening. Many clients I have worked with have full-on anxiety attacks triggered by driving. This over-functioning aspect of the brain, while protective in nature, can cause freezing and avoidance. Furthermore, repetitive stress responses contribute to health issues like high blood pressure, brain changes, insomnia, and even unhealthy coping mechanisms leading to self-destructive behaviors.

So what does courage have to do with fear? Courage allows us to act and move forward with something that scares us or causes us to feel vulnerable. It does not mean the absence of fear — it means action *amidst* fear. Taking even a small step toward your fear allows for growth and has the power to change lives, for avoidance becomes greater than the fear itself. Sometimes our biggest fears live inside the prison of our minds. Courage allows for an escape from the prison of anxiety and fear. Much of life ceases to exist without the courage to fully live authentically and from a place of vulnerability.

One of my all-time favorite songs, "Landslide" by Stevie Nicks, speaks of having to make changes after building a world around someone. Whether facing a divorce, a change in career, or something even smaller, such as starting a new school, courage allows us to listen to our hearts and step out into the unknown to take a risk. While courage sounds exciting and powerful, it does not always involve comfort. In fact, courage does not find measurement in the outcome but rather the jump toward embracing discomfort. Regardless of the response or outcome, showing up and being seen exemplifies courage.

Embracing courage means allowing and becoming comfortable with fear. Pushing fear away through distraction or other numbing behaviors contributes

Challenge of the Week

Reflect on something that you feel anxious about that might require courage.

What feels scary about this situation?

What does this anxiety feel like in your body?

What beliefs do you have about the situation?

How can you challenge yourself to confront this fear this week?

to avoidance and leads to stagnation and staying stuck, often in a perpetual cycle of anxiety. I often use metaphors in therapy to help illustrate points. My favorite involves the beach ball in the water metaphor.

Suppressing or avoiding fear is like trying to sit on a beach ball in a pool. Most would wobble and move side to side, struggling to keep the ball underwater. Letting the ball just float around us allows for ease and more peace. Allowing our feelings, including fear, helps us confront scary situations without avoidance. Courage helps us allow our fears to float around us and even run toward what might feel scary. Nurturing courage involves having a mindset that allows for risk-taking and living fully.

Here are some wonderful considerations when contemplating courage.

- What exactly are you afraid of happening? I prefer to add, "and what does that mean?" when exploring this question. If what you are afraid of or avoiding happens, what would that mean? Keep asking this question until you get to the root of your fear.

- What would happen if you took a chance?

- What are you waiting for?

- Try to focus on the journey rather than the outcome or results. Think about learning or even celebrating taking the risk versus what happens.

- How does this fear limit you? What would life look like without this avoidance?

Top Ten Common Fears I Have Seen as a Counselor

This highly anecdotal list, not based on empirical research, comes from my clinical experience of more than twenty years working with anxiety and trauma. See if any of these fears resonate with you.

- Failing
- Not being good enough
- Being judged (looking foolish, stupid, etc.)
- Change
- Falling in love

- Sharing feelings
- Growth
- Success or happiness (enter self-sabotage)
- Abandonment/being alone
- Rejection

Think about areas in your life that require courage.
Fill in the squares below with examples from your life to help you
challenge your courage and overcome fear. I've provided an
example using social anxiety as inspiration.

Small	Big
Small/Unimportant	**Big/Unimportant**
Ordering food at a restaurant	Making a speech at a friend's wedding
	(unimportant in the sense that if you cannot do it, your friendship will not necessarily suffer)

Courage
Grid

Small/Important	**Big/Important**
Answering a question in class where participation counts toward grade	Speaking up about a safety concern at school

Unimportant

Important

The Inner Child Inside of Us

Children are natural Zen masters; their world is brand-new in each and every moment. For the unwounded child, wonder is natural. Life is a mystery to be lived. Homecoming is the restoration of the natural. Such a restoration is not grandiose or dramatic; it is simply the way life ought to be.

— JOHN BRADSHAW, *Homecoming: Reclaiming and Championing Your Inner Child*

In the 1980s, psychology's inner child movement involved discovering and reconnecting with our inner child through exploration and reflection by re-parenting our hurt and wounded child parts. This powerful concept states that each of us has a child version of ourselves that sometimes carries hurts and triggers from the past into the present.

Our inner child can influence our current relationships and choices in ways we might not even realize. Sometimes adults or even other children may have hurt us or created environments that felt unsafe or scary. Our inner child parts may have developed amazing ways to cope and protect the whole self. Reconnecting with our inner child allows for healing through giving our younger selves a voice when they may not have had one.

In today's therapeutic world, the current model for understanding these wounded child parts involves the evidence-based Internal Family Systems framework. Recognizing our whole self as having multiple parts that each serve an important function allows for integrated healing. Internal Family Systems works well in healing complex childhood trauma. I have found this framework extremely helpful in my work with dissociative identity disorder (formerly multiple personality disorder) clients.

Connecting with our inner child does not have to mean there has been trauma or abuse. Everyone can benefit from connecting with their inner child, as our core self, unadulterated by the world, develops during this time of innocence. Our inner child provides a glimpse into the origins of our creativity, passion, and joy.

As a little girl, I loved exploring the world around me while I played outside, often getting dirty and delighting in simple pleasures like mud, flowers, bugs, and watching clouds. Fueling up on *Mister Rogers' Neighborhood,* I would bravely go outside to forage the great bamboo forest (which only consisted of a small patch of bamboo), explore under rocks, search for tiny exotic treasures like potato bugs, or hunt in my mom's flower bed for little blue wildflowers (which were really weeds).

Reflecting on these childhood days brings a smile to my face. Behind the scenes, though, secrets and repressed feelings lurked below the surface, never to be spoken aloud until I became an adult. I kept these more traumatic experiences tucked away for no one, even myself, to know about. Always smiling and trying to please, I recall delighting in nature and moving my body in freedom and amazement, perhaps as an adaptive way to cope with or embrace this special part of myself.

My childhood self had many parts — from playful, creative, adventurous, kind, shy, helpful, and wanting-to-please parts to suppressed parts that held fear, sadness, and anger. Connecting with my inner child became a powerful way for me to find healing and integrate these many parts that make up who I am today.

Our childhood can shape and influence us, and the inner child that lives within sometimes drives our current reality. Connecting with our inner child and re-parenting through support can allow

Getting to Know Your Inner Child

For each item below, list your favorite as a child.

Color: ....

Toy: ....

Friend: ....

Food: ....

Activity: ....

Game: ....

for deeper healing and guide us toward the needs that the adults in our lives might not have met. Hopefully, you experienced a happy childhood with mostly positive memories. However, some people may have few to no childhood memories or experienced abuse or trauma.

If you had a negative childhood, think about what you longed for or wished to have. Perhaps stability and consistency. Perhaps safety and security. Perhaps acceptance and unconditional love. Nurturing our inner child gives us a chance to provide that now, even if we didn't have it growing up. I can't think of anything more powerful in terms of a healing and corrective way to approach the past.

At times, learning the triggers of our inner children helps guide us along the healing journey. I often say that if you find yourself reacting above a six on a scale of zero to ten when others might respond at a lower level, old memories or feelings might have become triggered. Sometimes it's not even a highly traumatic memory, but suppressed and unprocessed emotions. This awareness can help us to tune in and check in with our inner child while responding differently in the present. If you resonate with the inner child concept, chances are your inner child needs some attention, and there's no one better to help that child than the adult you!

Regression Session

As a mom, I loved when my kids were little so I could make crafts or do activities that evoked my childhood nostalgia — activities like Shrinky Dinks®, Rainbow Loom®, and Pokémon® (which reminded me of Garbage Pail Kids cards from the 1980s).

Here's a list of ideas to have fun with that might engage your inner child. Feel free to add your own.

- Coloring books
- Crayons or colored pencils
- Stickers
- Play-Doh®
- Dolls
- Candy from the era you grew up in

Inner Child Healing through Nondominant Hand Journaling

This is one of my favorite therapeutic activities to connect with our inner children. It's adapted from Lucia Cappachione's book *Recovery of Your Inner Child*.[9] In this exercise, you'll use your nondominant hand to draw a picture of yourself as a young child, your "inner child." Then you'll dialogue with him or her using your right and left hands. The dominant hand will represent you as the adult, and the nondominant hand (yes, you will write with this) will be for your inner child. Don't worry, your handwriting is supposed to look messy like a child's, and perhaps, if you're like me, you might even stick out your tongue!

In the space below, use your nondominant hand to draw a picture of yourself as a child. You can use different colors or one color.

Now, in the space below, with your dominant hand, write a greeting to your child just as you would if you encountered a small child, such as "Hi, my name is Megan. What is your name? What is your favorite color?" Have your inner child answer using your nondominant hand. Continue chatting back and forth with your inner child like this as long as you'd like — if needed, grab some extra paper to continue the exercise!

Wholeness for Broken Hearts

Grief does not change you, Hazel.
It reveals you.

— JOHN GREEN, *The Fault in Our Stars*

As we continue to nurture ourselves during springtime, it makes sense to consider how painful endings often precede new beginnings. This season offers the opportunity to consider how to nurture the broken heart that comes from a relationship ending.

Losing a relationship or feeling rejection, abandonment, or unrequited love hurts physically and emotionally. Nurturing a broken heart requires tenderness, self-compassion, and courage through finding that missing piece to add to wholehearted healing. Building a support tribe through nurturing connections and practicing self-care allows for opportunities to create wholeness and restoration. If you're lucky, through introspection and deeper reflection, you might even learn lessons about yourself and healthy relationships in the process of mending your broken heart. Blessings really do come in disguise, though the

healing can feel messy, never-ending, and painful.

Think about a time you experienced a broken heart from a breakup or rejection from a romantic partner. What do you remember from this time? Perhaps feeling rejected, not being good enough, loneliness, or immense sadness. A breakup can trigger strong chemical responses in our brains, creating physical symptoms like that deep painful constriction in the chest, making it hard to breathe. A broken heart truly and literally hurts. In fact, a medical condition called "broken heart syndrome," or stress-induced cardiomyopathy, comes from sudden emotional distress and weakens the heart muscles, causing symptoms like a heart attack with pain, chest tightness, and shortness of breath.

Understanding neurobiology helps us to make sense of and become more empowered in healing a broken heart. Hormones like oxytocin and neurotransmitters like dopamine and serotonin impact bonding, pleasure, and mood. Oxytocin, the love hormone, allows for those warm feelings of connection and bonding that come from being in love or with sexual intimacy. A breakup literally causes a drop in this love hormone, creating physical withdrawal-like symptoms. Dopamine, the neurotransmitter responsible for pleasure, and even serotonin, a neurotransmitter responsible for positive mood and sleep, also play a role. These shifts and changes create both physiological and emotional responses experienced during a heartbreak.

Three Tips for Recovering from a Heartbreak

Find your tribe (oxytocin). Find other alternatives besides contact with an ex-partner for bonding. This allows the brain to reset its oxytocin levels to prevent chasing this chemical or going through relapses. Having contact with an ex and getting higher oxytocin levels only to break up and go through withdrawal again creates that never-ending on-again, off-again cycle, prolonging healing.

Find pleasurable things to do (dopamine). Consider learning something new by taking a class like belly dancing. Or find ways to exercise, as this allows for natural changes in the brain like higher dopamine levels. Find ways to create excitement. I once went skydiving! While you don't have to do something that extreme, make a change like a new hairstyle or try a sport.

Practice self-care (serotonin). Find ways to practice self-soothing through engaging your mindfulness muscle and your five senses, like taking a hot bubble bath, going for a walk outside in nature, or petting an animal. Practice a routine with good sleep habits, as discussed in the winter season section (see page 45).

I often share the wound metaphor with patients when doing heavy emotional work in therapy. Think of healing the loss, trauma, or emotional pain as treating a gaping wound. The first step is stopping the bleeding with emergency efforts like boundaries (no contact with an ex, changing the environment or routine). Sometimes, due to defense mechanisms like denial and suppression, the heartbroken can engage in self-destructive or reckless behaviors or engage in rebound relationships, making the wound worse or infected.

Next comes the cleaning and bandaging stage. This part is the hardest and can feel quite painful, as it requires digging around and applying some stinging medications like feeling uncomfortable emotions, finding healthy ways to express feelings, and self-soothing.

Finally, a scab will form, only to be ripped off suddenly by life's triggers, delaying the healing process. Perhaps an ex-partner starts dating someone new or seems happy on social media, or you encounter another loss of some sort. While mostly healed, a scab can become reinfected without proper care. Limiting social media or refocusing on yourself by connecting with a support system can help keep the scab in place while protecting the wound to ensure healing.

Eventually, a scar forms, and, when looking down, you can recall the event that caused the wound without experiencing as much pain. Seeing the scar might stir up memories or emotions, but the wound, now fully healed, can allow for life to move forward.

❁ Comfort First Aid Kit ❁

Make a comfort first aid kit by listing the things that can help when you feel heartbreak or sadness. Include items that help build your tribe, self-soothe, express feelings, and offer a healthy distraction when needed.

....

....

....

....

Express Yourself

What does it feel like for you personally to have a broken heart? Try to find song lyrics, a poem, or even some lines of movie dialogue that reflect your feelings. Then, write them in the broken heart below to help yourself heal.

WEEK
20

Mother Earth in the World Around Us

When the last tree is cut, the last fish is caught, and the last river is polluted; when to breathe the air is sickening, you will realize, too late, that wealth is not in bank accounts and that you can't eat money.

— ALANIS OBOMSAWIN

Springtime seems the perfect season for celebrating and nurturing our relationship with Mother Earth. While some might embrace our planet's spiritual, scientific, metaphorical, or even literary personification, appreciating our earth becomes a universal task for all humans as we rely on our planet and biosphere for survival. Our earth offers special gifts through the splendors and beauty found in nature, ultimately helping us find meaning and a connection with something greater. No matter your beliefs about creation, all of life centers on the habitability of our planet.

Finding ways to show respect, care, and protection of natural resources, from the oceans teeming with marine life, to the air we breathe, to the energy beneath our earth's crust and from the sun, will ensure healthy balance and life for future generations to come.

With reverence and respect for the land and the cyclical nature of the seasons, many Indigenous and Native cultures find meaning in nature. The Greek goddess of earth, Gaia, gives her name to Mother Gaia as she helps balance and promote the habitability of our land, seas, and biosphere. Just like us, our home planet deserves our love, nurturing, and reverence.

Whether you consider yourself a Greta Thunberg who prefers to engage in activism or environmentalism, or you find yourself enjoying the amazing splendor and glory of Mother Nature's artwork through time spent outdoors, it makes sense to extend consideration for ways to honor and show appreciation to the world around us. In our world, nature tends to have a way of reminding us of her power through storms and natural disasters, as well as through the many wonders of the world like canyons, waterfalls, mountains, deserts, valleys, and oceans.

Engaging in recycling efforts, conservation of water, and limiting our carbon footprint through measures like vegetarianism or electric cars can have lasting impacts upon our world.

Honor Mother Nature

Consider a simple change you can make in your life to help nurture our planet. Try to commit to this behavior through a daily or weekly schedule, or organize a trash pickup event at the beach or on a neighborhood road.

I will show my respect for Mother Earth by:

Sunday

Monday

Tuesday

Wednesday

Thursday

Friday

Saturday

Showing appreciation for the environment through taking action could lead to even greater change if all humans participated. There is nothing sadder to me than seeing trash line a road or wash up on the beach.

Our appreciation for Mother Earth can extend to our mindfulness practice.

Often while busy and distracted, surrounded by man-made sounds, machines, and smells, we become disconnected and distant from nature.

I feel most grounded to myself and my spirituality when in nature. Something amazing happens when I walk on the beach, tasting the salty air and feeling

Engage Your Senses

Spend some time outside delighting in Mother's Earth's beauty and the gifts she provides us. Share about your experience here in full sensory detail.

What did you see? Think about colors, shapes, animals, plants, sky.

....

....

....

....

....

What did you hear? Think about the sounds of nature versus man-made sounds.

....

....

....

....

....

....

....

the cool breeze with the warm sunlight, listening to the waves crash and the seagulls squeal. I become instantly renewed and restored just breathing fresh air and feeling the glory of Mother Earth's power in the ocean waves and sea breeze.

While I'm thankful to live near the beach, I long for the days when I can hike in a cool, damp forest, smelling the earthy dirt and trees and listening to the sound of rustling leaves beneath my feet and above my head as the wind blows through the trees. The mountains feel like home to me, offering a peaceful quiet and the powerful, collective, universal calling of my ancestors.

What did you smell? Consider the earthy smells around you.

....

....

....

What did you feel? Describe the temperature from the air, sunlight, or wind and the textures you felt.

....

....

....

What did you taste? Imagine any special tastes from plants, precipitation, etc.

....

....

....

The Inner Deity in Our Human Self

*How would you behave if you knew you were
a God or Goddess? How would you treat yourself?
How would you treat others? What kind of consciousness
would you hold about your smallest actions
if you knew their effects influenced the rest of creation?*

— ANODEA JUDITH, *Eastern Body, Western Mind:
Psychology and the Chakra System as a Path to the Self*

Each of us has gifts and qualities that make us unique and special. A deeper introspection allows us to find and nurture our gifts and internal strengths.

For those who have a faith-based perspective in life, many spiritual beliefs center around ascended masters, saints, gods, and goddesses that possess certain qualities and abilities that make them special and powerful. Nurturing our inner god or goddess for the purposes of this workbook is not meant to be taken literally per se, but more as a metaphor to help nurture those special spiritual qualities inside each of us. If you do not resonate with the goddess/god terminology, feel free to replace it with superheroes from Marvel movies, key characters from history, or aspects within your specific faith that resonate more personally.

Nurturing our inner goddess/god means connecting with the divine aspects within each of us as we recognize our own divine feminine and divine masculine parts. In the Asian worldview, yin and yang represent this duality. Feminine energy tends to hold space, provide softness, and flow, embracing the natural world and cycles in life. Masculine energy focuses on action and change, fueling success and achievement. Combining this energy allows for inner peace and balance, as we need both aspects in life.

Nurturing our inner divinity does not mean developing an exaggerated or inflated sense of self, hoping others will worship us. Rather, knowing our divinely inspired inner gifts and strengths and nurturing those internal qualities that make us special allows us to shine our light outward in the world. I imagine the world would radically change if we all recognized our inherent worthiness and nurtured our gifts so we could share them in the world to make a difference for the good of humanity.

Below is a list of some ascended masters, saints, and deities. Consider their qualities that you might appreciate or see within yourself or those that you would like to develop further.

Ascended Spiritual Masters

Guan Yin: Chinese goddess of love, peace, and healing

Jesus Christ: Regarded by Christians as the incarnation of God

Joan of Arc: French heroine and saint known for her fierce bravery in battle and beliefs

Fatima: Muslim daughter of the prophet Mohammed known for purity, chastity, and charity

Ganesh: Hindu god of new beginnings; remover of obstacles

White Buffalo Calf Woman: Sacred supernatural woman in Lakota bringing hope, abundance, harmony

Mother Teresa: Saint known for her selflessness and helping the poor

Buddha: Spiritual leader of enlightenment gained from morality, meditation, and wisdom

Oya: Goddess of the Yoruba tribe in Nigeria of the wind, thunder, and fire; she is known for her fierceness and protectiveness

So how do we tune in to and develop this inner divine superpower? Our Western world already values the action-focused masculine energy that drives independence, success, and achievement. So embracing the metaphor of our inner yin/yang balance, and finding ways to support our feminine energy, regardless of gender, makes sense. Let's consider some ways to nurture our inner divine goddess.

1. **Finding your tribe and others that support and nurture you.** This might involve a conscious decision to shift your energy to those that fill you up in different ways and do not drain you.

2. **Boundary-setting or letting go of toxic and unhealthy people or situations.** Ending relationships with people who disguise support with negativity or critical judgments in a false attempt to help can allow a new opening to develop a true support system.

3. **Letting go of negative self-talk and judgment.** Divine feminine energy often consists of holding space with acceptance and nonjudgment, allowing for life's natural flow. Allowing emotions and circumstances to unfold naturally without judgment and negativity helps us resist self-sabotage, numbness, and distraction efforts to avoid discomfort.

Divine Qualities

Divine Feminine/ Yin/Goddess	Divine Masculine/ Yang/God
Flow	Action
Holding space	Making changes
Acceptance	Resistance through strength
Wisdom	Achievement and success

Finding My Inner God
or Goddess

Draw a picture of your inner god or goddess in the space below. Be sure to include the qualities that make you special and how this might show up in the world. Consider unique traits, spiritual gifts, talents, and interests, as well as areas that you might want to develop. What do you notice about your inner divine being? How do you allow this part to shine in the world?

The Meaning of Life in Questioning Hearts

If there is a meaning in life at all, then there must be a meaning in suffering. Suffering is an ineradicable part of life, even as fate and death. Without suffering and death, human life cannot be complete.

— VIKTOR FRANKL, *Man's Search for Meaning*

As new beginnings bloom around us during the springtime months, the age-old existential ponderings about the meaning of life beckon. Reflecting upon this question helps us find purpose and meaning in our lives, especially during difficulties. Exploring meaning involves recognizing that something greater than ourselves exists. Perhaps you find yourself rooted in a specific religion. Maybe you consider yourself simply spiritual. Or perhaps you place high value in science and do not believe in a higher power.

Knowing your beliefs and contemplating life's ponderings can help create a foundation of meaning to help nurture the time we have here on earth in our human bodies and to reach beyond what cannot be explained rationally.

Studies show that people who believe their lives have meaning have a greater sense of well-being than those who don't. A 2019 study referenced in an article in *The Atlantic* found that the statement "I have a philosophy of life that helps me understand who I am" connects to lower rates of depression.[10] As a therapist, I have found in my anecdotal experience that those with a stronger faith-based belief system find more comfort or reassurance when dealing with life's struggles or anxiety, particularly when related to fear of death, grief, or managing trauma and suffering.

As a hospice social worker, I had the honor of sitting with people as they entered the dying process, ultimately leading to the last breath of life. I found this experience truly sacred. While I don't know for sure what happens after death, this exposure to the dying process helped propel me on a quest for deeper reflection on the meaning of life.

In 1967, Dr. Ian Stevenson founded the Division of Perceptual Studies at the University of Virginia's School of Medicine Psychiatry Department. Through research, this group delves into empirically-based studies suggesting that consciousness survives death and that the mind and brain are distinct and separate. Our mainstream scientific and philosophical beliefs often point to brain activity ending at death. Further studies into quantum physics, energy, near-death experiences, and consciousness open the door to many possibilities that the mind, body, and spirit are interconnected yet distinct.

While some might enjoy studying and learning about the meaning of life from a scientific perspective, others might find comfort and peace in their religion's traditional practices and tenets. Spirituality practiced through religion creates a sacred way to explain our human world's supernatural and unpredictable nature. Religion and spirituality offer hope and meaning and create an order in which to practice our faith-based beliefs.

When contemplating the meaning of life within different belief systems,

Diversity in Faith

What experiences have shaped your personal belief system and understanding of spirituality?

What faith do you align with currently in your life?

How might your faith have been different if you had grown up in a different family, state, or country?

In your knowledge of faiths other than your own, where do you see common teachings or beliefs that align with your personal beliefs?

some people might feel anxiety about choosing correctly. For others, roots in religious or spiritual practices and beliefs introduced during childhood create a strong solid foundation. Perhaps the real meaning of life involves each individual walking through his or her own spiritual journey.

Interestingly, a model of psychotherapy, called logotherapy, exists to analyze and determine the meaning of a patient's life. Founded by Victor Frankl, a survivor of Nazi concentration camps and the author of the book *Man's Search for Meaning,* logotherapy involves the connection to finding meaning amidst suffering. Through his experiences in a concentration camp, Frankl found survival happens in the context of hope and the ability to transcend suffering and misery through having a sense of control that comes from choosing what you believe. Seeing other prisoners offer kindness and support to one another was a true testimony to the human spirit, in choosing to focus on goodness and what was within their control under such horrific conditions.

Frankl's logotherapy consists of the basic belief that meaning comes from the individual's inner resources and core self. While logotherapy seeks to find meaning and purpose, Frankl noted that it ensures neither ensure happiness nor comfort. When contemplating the meaning of life, meaning happens amidst the suffering.

Logotherapy Principles

1. Mind, body, spirit: Our spirit is who we are and our identity (not theologically based).

2. There is meaning even in suffering.

3. Humans have a will to find meaning, which becomes the motive for living.

4. We are free to find meaning no matter how negative the circumstances.

5. The meaning of each moment leads to alignment with values or conscience.

6. Individuals are unique.

Explore Your Faith

Take some time to explore these beliefs regarding your faith.

What happens after you die?

Where do we come from?

What is the meaning of suffering?

Does life exist beyond earth?

How do science and faith intersect?

Does evil exist?

What are our relationships with other living beings?

A New Perspective in Trapped Minds

There is a huge amount of freedom that comes to you when you take nothing personally.

— DON MIGUEL RUIZ, *The Four Agreements: A Practical Guide to Personal Freedom*

Most people have experienced negative automatic thoughts that swirl around in our brains and hijack our emotions and experiences. In the 1960s, Dr. Aaron Beck developed the cognitive behavioral approach for addressing such common thinking distortions.

Finding a more positive or helpful perspective allows trapped and stagnant negative thoughts to fall away. A new perspective can help create a sense of control over situations, no matter how uncomfortable or difficult. Common distorted thought patterns contribute to a negative interpretation and then an emotional reaction based upon this distorted belief. It is the meaning placed on the event, rather than the action, situation, or experience, that contributes to the thought and emotion.

Consider an example of having an automatic negative thought. Perhaps you smile and say hello to a person who walks by you at the office, but they do not acknowledge you. The first thought entering your mind may be "I guess they don't like me." Full of assumptions, this thought has the power to contribute to feelings of insecurity and self-consciousness. But alternative explanations exist — perhaps they didn't see you because they were zoning out and not paying attention. Or maybe they felt shy or socially anxious and avoided eye contact.

Recognizing automatic negative thoughts creates the opportunity to change

Ten Common Cognitive Distortions[11]

1. **Mind reading:** Thinking you know what someone else is thinking without evidence. "I bet she doesn't like me" or "He thinks I'm stupid."

2. **Overgeneralizing:** Taking a single event or situation and applying it to all situations. The key word is "always" or "never." Getting rejected once and thinking, "I always get rejected."

3. **Catastrophizing:** Thinking about the worst-case scenario, often snowballing in nature. You get a failing grade on one math test and think you will fail out of school and not get into college.

4. **Minimizing:** Opposite of catastrophizing. Taking something that is a big deal and acting like it doesn't matter. Someone compliments you on a promotion, and you say, "Oh, it's no big deal, everyone gets promoted."

5. **Discounting the positive:** Ignoring positive information and focusing only on the negatives of a situation. A goalie makes five saves but only focuses on the one miss.

6. **Fortune-telling:** Thinking you know what will happen in the future with no evidence. "I know that she will say no, so I'm not even going to ask."

7. **Emotional reasoning:** Having an emotion and thinking it is the truth about a situation. Feeling lonely and thinking, "I'm a loser with no friends."

8. **Labeling:** Putting a label on a situation or feeling. Not being invited to a party and calling yourself a "loser."

9. **Polarizing:** Thinking in terms of extreme ends of a spectrum without considering the middle ground. You think of yourself as bad or good, fat or skinny, smart or stupid, fun or boring.

10. **Should-ing:** Telling yourself what you should or shouldn't be doing, creating feelings of shame. Or telling someone else what they should do or not do, creating boundary issues.

unhelpful thoughts using defusing statements or questions. Challenging cognitive distortions brings more balanced perspective and ease in life.

The first step to finding a new perspective involves detaching from the negative thoughts rather than fully challenging them. Sometimes the attempt to determine if a thought is true or untrue causes the thought to become stuck and get more attention than necessary. As a metaphor, imagine giving attention to a dog engaging in a behavior you do not like. Trying to figure out why the dog engages in this behavior, whether you ask in a pleasant tone or scolding tone, may unintentionally reinforce the dog to continue the behavior by giving more attention and interaction. The same can be said about giving undue attention to negative thoughts.

Ultimately, our reality comes from our thoughts, both helpful and unhelpful.

Thoughts deeply influence feelings and actions as each emotion connects with urges to act. Sometimes rather than give a thought attention, even by challenging the thought, it helps to pivot focus to a more helpful belief. For instance, if the thought "I never get invited to parties" comes to my mind, you could use mindfulness skills first to notice you are having the thought without challenging or correcting the statement. Using this technique, you would simply take note of the thoughts circulating in your brain. They simply become words in your mind, nothing more and nothing less. Words and thoughts are just words and thoughts. The power comes from noticing and observing without placing meaning or having to act. Calling a thought just a thought allows for detachment from the meaning of the thought. Suspending meaning allows more control and power over the mind.

Helpful Thought Challenges

- What evidence is there for or against this belief?
- Is there another way to look at this situation?
- What would a friend tell me? What would I tell a friend if they had this belief?
- Will this matter tomorrow, next month, next year, on my deathbed?
- When has this thought not been true?

Noticing Cognitive Distortions

Complete the following chart with a situation that happened this week.
Fill in your first thought, how you feel, and your response. Then check to see
if you might be thinking with a cognitive distortion and if there might be
a more helpful thought. Repeat this exercise in a separate journal
whenever you want to examine your thought patterns.

Event:

Initial
Thought:

Initial
Feeling:

Response/
Action:

More Helpful
Thought:

Authenticity in a Follow-Me World

You'll learn, as you get older, that rules are made to be broken. Be bold enough to live life on your terms, and never, ever apologize for it. […] Laugh in the face of adversity. […] March to the beat of your own drummer. And stubbornly refuse to fit in.

— MANDY HALE, *The Single Woman: Life, Love, and a Dash of Sass*

One of my top three values in life involves authenticity. Being genuine in our world seems a rarity considering the age of social media and the endless ways to conform to outside standards and pressure to keep up with others. Rooted in truth, authenticity blooms outward in the genuine expression of personality and spirit.

Consider for a moment the many ways denial of our authentic self happens. Perhaps following the current beauty standards or trends, staying in an unfulfilling job to meet others' expectations, or pretending to like others to fit in. I thought people grew out of this after completing the developmental task of finding identity in adolescence. But many adults continue to deny their authentic selves and find themselves copying and pasting to keep up with others. To be honest, nurturing authenticity doesn't come easily. It takes intention, self-awareness, and courage to move beyond external influences on our self-worth.

Think about someone you know who exemplifies authenticity. What do you notice about this person? Perhaps they speak their truth even if this goes against what others believe. Perhaps they dress or talk in a way that differs from most people. Most authentic people I know have a sense of knowing who they are, and what they like and don't like, and have more mature defense mechanisms like humor or altruism to cope with difficulties. Authentic people have matured and evolved past the fitting-in stage and focus more on being true to themselves, even amidst the potential for judgment or rejection.

One of my favorite ways authenticity shows up involves the ability to apologize and take responsibility for making a mistake. Deflecting or making excuses for poor behavior pulls us away from truth, creating inauthenticity and dishonesty. Owning up to our flaws and imperfections when making a mistake requires a sense of self-worth, because extending grace to others and ourselves paves the way to understanding and openness.

Authentic people find purpose and meaning within themselves. Whether living congruently within their belief system or aligning their life to reflect their personal values, authentic people neither pretend nor go along with the masses. They stay true to their beliefs and internal knowing.

An important consideration in nurturing authenticity involves learning to set boundaries. Placing others' needs and wants above our own to pursue worthiness and acceptance destroys our sense of self. Denying ourselves through not speaking up, avoiding conflict, and people-pleasing leads to resentment and ultimately feels like a slow death as we slip further from authenticity.

Sometimes when talking about setting boundaries, people focus only on meeting their own needs or wants, no longer considering another person's feelings in the name of setting boundaries. As with most things in life, boundary-setting works best in the context of balance. For instance, I consider myself empathic and kindhearted. I enjoy helping others, not from a sacrificial quest for my

My Authenticity Tribe

Consider who knows the real, uncensored you. Think about what allows you to be your true self within these relationships. What qualities do you look for in creating a tribe that will nurture and support you in sharing your authentic self?

self-worth, but more from recognizing my inherent gifts and strengths. As a healer, my authentic self cares deeply for others. To honor my authenticity, I must incorporate this caring and love for deep and meaningful connections while balancing boundary-setting to protect my energy so I can continue to live authentically within my values of helping others.

Authenticity does not mean only caring about yourself. It means being true to yourself. You can care for and nurture others, particularly if this is part of your authentic self. There is a warning to heed, though: When you are fully authentic and genuine, some people will not like you. As a recovered people pleaser, I have learned to let go of others' opinions of me. It's a little easier once you've made it past forty!

Authenticity Inventory

Read each statement below and think about how much or little it applies to you. How does your sense of authenticity connect with each idea?

- I generally share my beliefs and opinions openly with others no matter the situation.
- I prefer to dress in a way that reflects my personality, likes, or interests.
- I am a follower of different trends or of others.
- I change my clothing to fit in with others.
- Everyone likes me.
- I hide my true feelings and thoughts for fear of judgment or rejection.
- I value my unique sense of humor.
- Others don't really know me.
- I do not listen to my inner voice or follow my gut instincts.
- I change who I am depending on whom I am around.

Personal Mission Statement

Many businesses have mission statements to help them focus on aligning and operating within their ideals. Creating a personal mission statement is a fun, tried-and-true activity for nurturing authenticity. Think about the below guidelines and then form your own personal mission statement. Write it in the box below.

1. Identify three to five core values that are important to you (see page 24). Describe how these values might show up in your life. For instance, if you value authenticity, perhaps you make a point to allow your sense of humor to show.

2. Consider how you plan to use your gifts and strengths in the world.

3. Think about what matters to you in life. What brings you joy?

4. Our mission can evolve and change throughout time. Consider what used to be important to you and how that has changed. Think about what matters to you now.

5. Consider the lasting impact you want to leave on the world. How will you want others to remember you?

My Mission Statement

Manifestation in Knowing Hearts

*Ask for what you want and
be prepared to get it!*

— MAYA ANGELOU

Earlier, we talked about dreams and vision boards. So how is manifesting different? Paying attention to our inner thoughts and what we speak aloud helps focus attention on what matters in life. Often what becomes spoken aloud becomes a reality, as this subconsciously stored information has the power to influence behaviors and choices.

Operating from a fear-based or negative mindset that things won't work out creates a template for reality called a self-fulfilling prophecy. While conscious and subconscious beliefs influence choices and behaviors, a self-fulfilling prophecy predicts and then cyclically creates the future. If we embrace the self-fulfilling prophecy model, it makes sense to keep our beliefs and thoughts about the future positive. For instance, thinking, "I'm never going to have any money" might manifest itself by laying a foundation for a belief that having money becomes impossible. This might influence decisions consciously or subconsciously in denying opportunities or making choices out of fear or a lack mindset.

Manifesting has become more popular in recent years. For some, manifesting has a more spiritual connotation, as in a person having a higher vibration of calming energy can manifest something through positively envisioning and creating energy as if this positive event has already happened. The law of attraction in which what you put out in the universe comes back to you is central to this belief. No matter the perspective, though, thinking more positively makes sense in allowing ourselves to stay focused on our goals and desires. It feels empowering to believe we have some influence and control over our lives.

A complete focus on the positive starts to sound a little like toxic positivity, a superficial, albeit more comfortable, way to gloss over suffering. Toxic positivity is similar to magical thinking. Magical thinking describes a superstitious belief a child might have that they can control an outcome by engaging in a behavior. For example, "Don't step on a crack, or you'll break your mother's back." As a child, I used magical thinking when I had to kiss every stuffed animal in my room goodnight so nothing bad would happen to me when I slept. I believed it wholeheartedly as a way to avoid uncomfortable feelings and fears. Do you have any magical thinking, even as an adult? I do like to sleep with my toes under the blankets so no one will eat them.

I point this out to help understand that sometimes negative beliefs or uncomfortable feelings serve a purpose and can help prompt us into action. If I think I will fail my test, I might study more the night before. If I only applied the manifesting concept, however,

❀ Speak It into Existence ❀

What do you want for your life? Create a simple statement and then visualize it happening. Perhaps find an object or a symbol to represent this manifestation and come back to it from time to time to focus on your manifestation. The key in practicing this involves imagining what you want as if it has already happened. Rather than wishing, hoping, or wanting, you envision and create it as reality in your manifesting mind. Have fun and see what happens and where it goes.

Dream it. Believe it. Live it.

....

....

....

....

I would imagine passing my test as if it would happen simply because I believed it or put it out there. Blindly releasing any negative beliefs or worry might cause me to play video games rather than study. Some uncomfortable feelings help prompt positive action.

Similarly, only focusing on the positive might be invalidating when experiencing trauma or suffering. Sometimes bad things happen in life, regardless of the thought or mindset. External forces over which we have no control, including other people or events, influence outcomes. Placing too much emphasis on the positive mindset can simplify and minimize the significance of external events in affecting our reality.

Best Manifestation Practices

Manifestation Done Well	Manifestation Done Unhealthily
Taking a minute before a test begins to visualize yourself succeeding on it, putting yourself into a positive mindset	Visualizing yourself succeeding on a test the night before instead of studying
Starting your morning with a brief ritual of repeating your goals out loud	Obsessively consuming mantra YouTube videos
Visualizing the excitement of winning a soccer game	Thinking about the other team being better to try to motivate yourself to work harder and feeling anxious
Imagining people liking you and inviting you to hang out	Sitting by the phone waiting and waiting for someone to reach out to you

After reflecting on manifestation practices, consider the ways manifesting can play a role in your life and how you can incorporate this more into your daily activities.

My Manifestations Log

Consider some areas in your life that you would like to manifest into existence and come up with a helpful belief. Also write down an unhelpful, negative belief so you can identify unhealthy ways to manifest in contrast with the healthy ways. Keep a log to see if your manifestations work!

	Unhelpful (negative)	Helpful (neutral to positive)	Outcome
EXAMPLE	I need to get a B on a test to pass the course. I hope I can do that.	I am able to get at least a B on this test.	I got a good grade!
EXAMPLE	This team is better than us. I hope we can win.	I know we can win. We are better than this team.	Even though we didn't win, we worked hard and didn't give up.

WEEK
26

Grace in Forgiving Hearts

Grace doesn't depend on suffering to exist, but where there is suffering you will find grace in many facets and colors.

— WM. PAUL YOUNG, *The Shack*

As a lifelong United Methodist, learning about John Wesley's understanding of grace helped shape my understanding of extending forgiveness to others. Wesley, the founder of the Protestant Methodist movement, wrote about how God's grace influences our lives. But you need not be Christian or have any religious or spiritual affiliations to appreciate the richness and fullness offered through experiencing and extending grace. The Merriam-Webster dictionary defines grace as "disposition to or an act or instance of kindness, courtesy, or clemency." Imagine what would happen in the world if we extended this kind of grace to others!

Grace requires preparing the heart and mind to allow its spirit to move through us and into the world around us. Grace, to me, evokes feelings of peace and serenity in finding acceptance and letting go of anger, sadness, and fear. Forgiveness involves moving through different stages, ultimately ending in a complete surrender and release of burden.

Consider for a moment a time in your life when someone or something caused you hurt or pain. Perhaps this was rejection in a romantic relationship or an event in childhood. This hurt, tender and vulnerable, causes the natural tendency to protect oneself from getting hurt again. Feelings of anger, giving a sense of power and strength, help vulnerable hearts experiencing loss or shame. Forgiveness and grace can feel impossible sometimes when considering the suffering caused by another's actions.

As a therapist specializing in trauma, working with grace and forgiveness presents a challenge. Holding and creating a safe space for homicide, suicide, or childhood abuse survivors involves allowing full expression of a range of feelings, from devastation, loss, and anger to sadness, despair, and fear. How can grace and forgiveness fit into the healing equation without invalidating or minimizing pain and suffering? Ultimately, grace comes not from reconciliation with another person but from releasing and letting go of the burden in our hearts and souls without harming another or ourselves.

In my practice, I have found healing, while nonlinear, moves through different phases toward a final letting go. Feelings of fear, violation, and betrayal surface when working with upsetting or traumatic events. Necessarily, the first stage involves creating a sense of safety through grounding in the present. Often sadness follows, while soothing the way through the loss of innocence and trust. Anger comes next, bringing with it a sense of injustice and feelings of revenge. This stage calls for finding ways to channel anger healthily, a critical component to healing.

A step that sometimes feels uncomfortable moves toward seeking to understand. This in no way excuses the person causing pain. Work in this stage must happen gently and intuitively. Delving deeper into understanding how something happens can help create more awareness and empower healing. Extending forgiveness and grace inward

A Therapeutic Process for Grace

1. Create safety and practice grounding and mindfulness skills.

2. Explore vulnerable feelings of fear, hurt, and sadness through self-soothing.

3. Allow for anger and find healthy ways to express feelings related to injustice and betrayal.

4. Seek understanding of the person causing the hurt, or from a larger perspective, and engage in compassion.

5. Let go and release the burden and pain caused by extending forgiveness. This doesn't mean you need to share with or confront the person who hurt you.

and outward does not absolve the person who caused the suffering, but rather releases suffering for the hurting.

Another consideration when talking about grace involves extending ourselves forgiveness when we make mistakes. Holding onto feelings of shame can cause toxic behaviors and beliefs to fester and can turn into a never-ending cycle. For instance, when feeling shame, whether real or perceived, suppressing these feelings can create problems in relationships. Shame, an uncomfortable feeling, often becomes disguised and displaced as anger onto someone or something. Since we tend to protect ourselves from uncomfortable feelings, the resulting defensive behaviors to avoid shame ultimately create more shame, allowing the cycle to continue.

Guilt and shame differ slightly. The former stems from acting in a way that goes against our values and moral code. In contrast, shame comes from a core unworthiness belief. Put another way, typically, guilt comes from things we do, while shame comes from a belief of who we are. In therapy sessions, I often use the example of stealing a cookie from a cookie jar: guilt comes from stealing, which goes against my values; shame tells me I am a terrible person because I stole something. Guilt reminds us to stay on the right path by correcting our behaviors to align with our values. Internalized shame becomes toxic and fuels self-rejection, which can lead to numbing or destructive self-sabotaging behaviors.

Extending and nurturing internal grace is a critical step toward practicing self-compassion and gratitude to allow for full healing.

Understanding the Importance of Extending Self-Forgiveness and Grace

GUILT: This is what we feel when acting in a way that misaligns with our values, beliefs, or morals. Typically, this emotion can prompt us to make better choices.

SHAME: This is the internalized or externalized belief of being unworthy and undeserving.

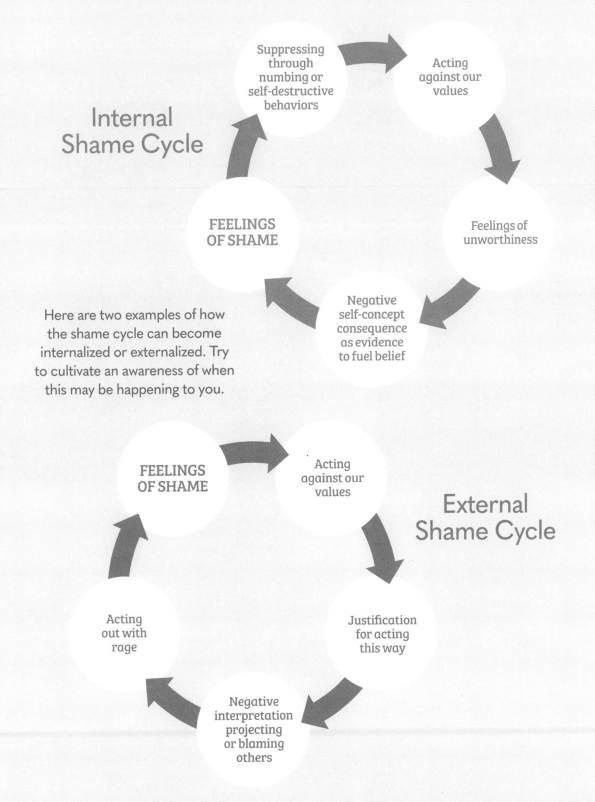

Internal Shame Cycle

- Suppressing through numbing or self-destructive behaviors
- Acting against our values
- Feelings of unworthiness
- Negative self-concept consequence as evidence to fuel belief
- FEELINGS OF SHAME

Here are two examples of how the shame cycle can become internalized or externalized. Try to cultivate an awareness of when this may be happening to you.

External Shame Cycle

- FEELINGS OF SHAME
- Acting against our values
- Justification for acting this way
- Negative interpretation projecting or blaming others
- Acting out with rage

Extending Grace and Forgiveness through Guided Letter Writing

For this exercise, think about someone who has hurt or caused you pain. Consider writing them a letter offering grace and releasing your pain and suffering. Then, in the second letter, try extending this same grace toward yourself for something you did.

Dear ....

I am writing to let you know that what you did hurt me.
I have held on to how you: ....

....

....

Your actions affected me in many ways as I dealt with what
happened. I found myself: ....

....

....

I felt: ....

....

....

I want you to know that I am choosing to no longer hold on to these
feelings anymore. I understand better that: ....

....

....

With grace,

....

Dear Me,

I am writing to let you know that what you did hurt me.
I have held onto how you: ....
....
....
....

Your actions affected me in many ways as I dealt with what
happened. I found myself: ....
....
....
....

I felt: ....
....
....
....

I want you to know that I am choosing to no longer hold on to these
feelings anymore. I understand better that: ....
....
....
....

With grace and love,

....

Body Positivity in Critical Minds

Pretty much the strongest, most badass, and rebellious thing that you can do is to love your body in this world that screams at you that you shouldn't.

— LAURA BATES, *Girl Up*

Depending on where you live, as springtime fades to summer and bathing suit season looms ahead, feelings of discomfort and body shame can emerge. Nurturing body positivity becomes essential. Recently I checked off a bucket list item and had the opportunity to embrace my imperfect body by going to a nude beach. Yes, you read that correctly.

My experience prompted inner reflection on the opportunity to embrace my body completely, and I mean completely. I didn't gawk or stare, but I did delight in a new appreciation for the human form. Curvy, skinny, small, short, tall, muscular, attractive, unattractive, hairy, smooth, lumpy, bumpy, tight, loose, brown, dark brown, white, and red (sunscreen is a *must*). I quickly began to realize that it's the diversity in many bodies that becomes attractive, not the individual.

I'm sure I wouldn't have had the confidence to go to a nude beach in my early twenties, even with a more desirable body. Back then, insecurities and negative self-talk held me hostage, and it wouldn't have been fun or freeing. But this naked walk on the beach, while in my fattest, flabbiest, and oldest body, reflects my intentional work to nurture body acceptance. Learning to delight in the sensory experience and noticing your surroundings is one of the quickest ways to get out of your critical mind space and live fully in your body.

In the world of advertising and social media, body neutrality, much less body positivity, can be difficult to master.

Advertising highlights deficits so the consumer will buy beauty, health, or weight-loss products, while social media encourages comparing ourselves to others. These external forces require deeper work on correcting internal negative self-talk. Appreciating your body looks and sounds different than beating yourself up with critical chatter. Cutting out negative body shaming can go a long way in motivating self-acceptance.

✿ Helpful Body-Positive Talk ✿

Appreciate and reframe the negative body chatter below to more neutral or even positive beliefs.

For example, "My stomach is so fat and flabby." Instead, you could think, "My cat loves kneading my soft belly." Or, "My curves feel feminine. If I lived in the Renaissance era, I'd have the ideal shape."

My thighs are too fat: ....

....

I have too much cellulite: ....

....

I'm gross and disgusting: ....

....

Ugh, I'm too...: ....

....

I look bad in a bathing suit: ....

....

A key component to challenging negative beliefs about bodies involves intentionally changing the negative self-chatter. For most, this negative monologue happens instantaneously and unknowingly. Becoming more aware of our negative body talk offers the first opportunity to change. Sometimes a more positive thought or belief feels too unbelievable. It can help to find the neutral observation by sticking to facts. My thighs are large. My belly is soft. The negative meaning attached becomes the hijacker—words like gross, disgusting, ugly. Neutrality and observation allow us to suspend judgment so we can then decide to make positive change.

In my mid-thirties, after having children, my hormonal profile dramatically changed. I was officially diagnosed with polycystic ovarian syndrome (PCOS) and severe stage 4 endometriosis. PCOS wreaked havoc on my appearance and body confidence, and then, to my horror, I sprouted a full-blown goatee! Think dark, coarse hair, thicker than my husband's beard at the time. I desperately tried everything to deal with the hair, from multiple hair removal procedures to medications, supplements, and dietary changes. Nothing worked.

I decided I had two options: stay miserably self-conscious and consumed with trying to change this, or learn to accept the goatee. While I couldn't seem to fully control my weight issues or facial hair, learning to talk to myself more positively was something I *could* control. How empowering! While I must admit I'm not quite brave enough to walk around fully bearded, I have complete admiration and respect for women like body positivity model Harnaam Kaur, who does exactly this. Her bravery not only accepting but embracing her facial hair inspires other women to love themselves.

I recall once needing to run to the grocery store with my eight- and nine-year-old children. At the time, I hadn't shaved in a while, to show my physician the evidence of my beard. My children looked horrified that I would go into the store, so at that moment, I stopped the car, and we had an important chat about loving yourself for who you are, not what you look like, that physical appearance does not define a person, and that your worth does not come from other people's opinions. So, we marched up to that checkout line, my hairy chin held high, where I'm sure the young man on the register stared in awe, or perhaps disgust, or maybe he didn't even notice at all. But I didn't care either way. In that highly vulnerable moment, I had just modeled for my children what it means to love and accept yourself. It wasn't just talk—I showed them what it looks like, whiskers and all. Does chin hair mean that I'm unworthy or unattractive? Because honestly, what I find unattractive is selfishness, judging others, and shallowness.

YES	NO	
◯	◯	I wear clothes to hide my body.
◯	◯	I wear clothes to show off my body.
◯	◯	I usually wear comfortable clothing.
◯	◯	I check my reflection in the mirror or when I walk past a car or store window.
◯	◯	I talk negatively to the body parts I dislike.
◯	◯	I compare my body with others that I perceive as looking better.
◯	◯	I am critical and judge other bodies.
◯	◯	I restrict food intake to change my body.
◯	◯	I think about enhancing my body through surgery.
◯	◯	My appearance plays an important part in my self-worth.
◯	◯	I need makeup because I am ugly without it.
◯	◯	I use makeup as an art to express myself.
◯	◯	I am comfortable with others noticing me.

WEEK
28

Joy in Guarded Hearts

Sometimes your joy is the source of your smile, but sometimes your smile can be the source of your joy.

— THICH NHAT HANH

As the season warms, when children break from school and families begin to vacation, summertime, in shades of yellow, green, and blue, becomes the perfect time to focus on nurturing happiness. Happiness, one of the six primary emotions, comes from external situations or internal interpretations that create elevated feelings of excitement and delight.

Joy, often interchanged with happiness, carries with it a deeper connotation. Happiness, ebullient and bubbly, can feel like a jolt of electricity, while joy emerges more slowly, building a warmth of contentment from deep within; joy can simultaneously happen in the context of difficulties and challenges. I like to think of happiness as the hard candy coating to the tootsie roll surprise of joy.

For some, achieving happiness may feel like having arrived at completion. Some might even strive for perpetual happiness, though I often explain to clients that my definition of superior mental functioning comes from allowing a full range of emotions, not simply always feeling happy. As a result, I have never created a treatment plan with a goal for the patient to feel happier.

Allowing the full range of emotions means letting go of defenses designed to protect us from uncomfortable feelings. Allowing feelings to come and go while flowing through us creates more moments of happiness, as suppressing uncomfortable feelings disconnects and blocks all emotions. Trapping negative emotions in the mind's net creates a jammed-up mess, making it impossible to fully experience happiness as it is unable to pass through.

Brené Brown shares in her TED Talks "The Power of Vulnerability" about defense mechanisms and how they interact with vulnerability when describing that we "can't selectively numb uncomfortable feelings — instead, we numb all feeling."[12] So, to fully embrace and nurture happiness, we must allow all feelings. Numbing and distraction, while helpful in the short term and for crisis purposes when things feel too much to handle, become unhelpful when ignoring and avoiding long term. This new acceptance and appreciation of our emotions produce the contentment and happiness that come from allowing authentic vulnerability in fully living.

Stop and think for a moment about how many feelings you have already had today. If you're like me, you have probably experienced a range including perhaps boredom, irritation, excitement, anxiety, frustration, and amusement. Emotions move in and out the same way thoughts pop into and out of our minds. Learning to allow these feelings to flow fosters an atmosphere for a deeper, more stable mood state to develop.

The best way I can describe how to nurture joy involves piecing together moments of happiness while simultaneously honoring and labeling all feelings that emerge. While feelings are transient in nature, allowing them contributes to our ability to find meaning, take action, and connect. Emotions, housed in a specific region in the brain, have important functions, including validating experiences, prompting us into action, and communicating with others. Isn't it amazing that our brains have an entire region, called the amygdala, devoted to feeling and processing emotions?

Creating a Joy Chain

Nurturing joy in small moments allows for creating happiness. Often the search for happiness sounds elusive, proving challenging and overwhelming. Focusing on smaller moments allows for this to create a chain-like effect, adding more happiness to our lives.

Create a joy chain by focusing on things like animals, laughter, decorations, nature, the sky, human interaction, seeing acts of kindness, doing acts of kindness, food, or the sensory experience.

For those who feel their joy has dimmed, a conscious intention to improve the moment through perspective-shifting and mindfully connecting with themselves and the world around them can create a spark that can ignite into a full flame, fueling the reemergence of joy.

While talking about joy and happiness might make sense in creating a life worth living, the quest for happiness can sometimes become toxic in nature. Perpetually chasing happiness so we don't have to feel bad or uncomfortable creates opportunities for disconnection. This emotional shutoff can impact the ability to access empathy, which can negatively affect relationships and healthy coping skills.

Additionally, toxic positivity creates invalidation and shame for both the giver and receiver. If you're always seeking to spin things in a positive light to clean up someone's messy, uncomfortable feelings, the avoidance of negative feelings serves to squelch joy. As Kahlil Gibran wrote in *The Prophet,* "Some of you say, 'Joy is greater than sorrow,' and others say, 'Nay, sorrow is the greater.' But I say unto you, they are inseparable. Together they come, and when one sits alone with you at your board, remember that the other is asleep upon your bed."[13]

In nurturing joy, fully allowing the range of feelings from sorrow and suffering to peace and happiness creates a place of wholeness and alignment on what it means to become fully human.

Joy Thieves

Here's a list of common types of people that drain or steal happiness, joy, or contentment. Circle the ones that you can identify in your life (current or past), or think of some others of your own.

- Debbie Downers
- The Passive Aggressives
- The Entitled
- The Superficial
- Fake Friends
- Addictions

- Mindnumbers
- Deceitful Way
- Judgmental Judges
- The Narrowmindeds
- The Jealous

Chain of Joy

Identify events, people, places, or interests that activate feelings of happiness. Then, connect those with values important in your life to create joy. The aqua links are for the core values, and the pink links are for the concrete events and things that bring joy and relate to the core values. Notice how our values and things that bring us joy often align. What does your chain of joy look like?

EXAMPLE

Event: Listening to parents play music

Value: Family

Event: Learning to play crystal sound bowls

Value: Learning

Event: Going to a comedy show

Value: Humor

Event:
....
....

Value:
....
....

Event:
....
....

Value:
....
....

Event:
....
....

Value:
....
....

WEEK 29

Compassion for Others

*Too often we underestimate the power
of a touch, a smile, a kind word, a listening ear,
an honest compliment, or the smallest act of caring,
all of which have the potential to turn a life around.*

— LEO BUSCAGLIA

Sympathy means to feel for someone, while empathy means to feel with someone. Sympathy involves focusing on another's emotion from a distance, whereas empathy involves a full understanding by entering into another's reality. This allows for a deeper level of connection. Compassion involves taking action based on our feelings of empathy.

Those with high empathy often have high levels of compassion, which at times results in them overextending themselves. Healthy compassion, therefore, requires learning to set boundaries and practice regular self-care to avoid feeling too much.

Imagine the feelings that may come up if you were to encounter the following situations and how sympathy, empathy, and compassion might play a role: a homeless person sleeping on the street in cold weather; a parent who has experienced the death of a child;

a stray or injured animal; someone broken down on the side of the road; a child being bullied. If you're like me, your heart might already hurt. Others might have a more logical response or have opinions or beliefs related to these situations, creating different feelings than empathy. A few readers might overthink and need more details about the situation.

One challenge with empathy lies in our ability to tap into and allow uncomfortable and more vulnerable feelings. To feel sadness or compassion

Empathy Quiz

YES	NO	
◯	◯	I often become sad when seeing a stray animal, wanting to rescue it.
◯	◯	I do not make eye contact with other humans when walking on the street.
◯	◯	I feel bad if someone is unkind to a server or cashier.
◯	◯	If I see someone begging for money, I want to give them something.
◯	◯	When a child cries, I find it uncomfortable.
◯	◯	I can relate to others feeling sadness, injustice, or victimization.
◯	◯	I am uncomfortable with vulnerable feelings.
◯	◯	I cry at movies or while reading books.

for another, those feelings must become tolerable and accessible. As discussed in earlier chapters, defense mechanisms allow for blocks, helping prevent suffering. If you find this happening in yourself through minimizing, justifying, or blaming, just notice and explore the function of the defense. Chances are more vulnerable feelings might have become activated, interfering with an empathic or compassionate response.

It is important when talking about compassion to include a section on boundary-setting. Those who tend to have high levels of empathy often find themselves in unbalanced relationships where they give and do not receive the same back, at times leading to codependency or feeling used. While empathy means feeling with someone, it doesn't mean perpetually taking on the responsibility to fix another person's discomfort or challenges. This concept can prove difficult when having high levels of empathy or a value of compassion and must balance with self-care and boundaries.

Empathic individuals often have experienced traumatic situations in childhood. As a therapist working with childhood trauma, I have found many intuitive and empathic individuals develop a keen ability to read another person's mood or energy, even down to micro-expressions flitting across another's face. This stems from self-protection and a hypervigilance to know what might be coming next. *The Gift of Fear* by Gavin de Becker talks about this.[14] In order to protect themselves, survivors of trauma, particularly in childhood, become masters at feeling responsible for another's needs or desires.

For this reason, understanding trauma or unhealthy relationship patterns can help balance empathy and compassion, which becomes a beautiful gift in connecting and developing intimacy.

Empathy Aura

I like to think of our empathy as an energy field surrounding each of us. Those with higher empathy levels seem to have more holes in that energy field, allowing others' energy to become absorbed. Learning to set boundaries, as well as practice self-care, helps to desaturate from others' emotions. How can you fill in the holes to help practice self-care and set boundaries?

Take a Walk in Their Shoes

Imagine having empathy or compassion for someone whom you dislike or feel frustrated with at the moment. This exercise might be challenging — it's usually easy to empathize with someone we love — but it can really build the empathy muscle, though it is not meant to invalidate your feelings.

Describe the person and situation.

....

....

What do you think they might be feeling?

....

....

How do they struggle?

....

....

How do they show this?

....

....

How does this make you feel?

....

....

What action do you want to take?

....

....

WEEK
30

Passion in Bored Hearts

The saddest people I've ever met in life are the ones who don't care deeply about anything at all. Passion and satisfaction go hand in hand, and without them, any happiness is only temporary.

— NICHOLAS SPARKS, *Dear John*

Have you ever felt growing boredom or discontentment in life? The daily grind. Repetitive. Going through the motions. Life becomes stagnant and unfulfilling, with nothing to excite, inspire, or anticipate. Thankfully, you can learn to recognize the internal thoughts and external behaviors that indicate that you are devolving into the daily grind and on track to losing passion. Identifying and embracing passion allows us to then incorporate it into our lives.

When you hear the word *passion,* what comes to mind? Often associated with intense romantic feelings, desire, and an almost insatiable force outside of oneself, passion can evoke feelings of desire even to the point of tolerating any pain that might accompany it. In fact, passion comes from the Latin root word *patior,* which means to suffer.[15] Our modern use of the word involves a strong emotion forcing someone to act,

whether in love or hate. Passion implies a full heart without connection to the logical, rational mind.

Because passion can evoke strong emotions such as love, hate, rage, and desire, finding effective strategies to regulate and balance emotions helps when nurturing passion. One of my favorite explanations of finding balance in our minds involves the concept of Wise Mind, developed by Marsha

Linehan, the founder of dialectical behavior therapy.[16] She divides our mind into the rational and emotional mind, called Reasonable Mind and Emotional Mind. The Wise Mind comes from the intersection and balance between these two parts. Neither part holds negative or positive meaning, but the middle path between the two is the most effective place to land in most situations.

The Wise Mind

Think of a situation that balances the emotional and rational minds and share how Wise Mind would look and sound.

For example, someone rejects me on an online dating site.

EMOTIONAL MIND:
Hurt, rejected, unloved.

RATIONAL MIND:
Just because one person isn't interested in me doesn't mean I am unlovable or undesirable.

WISE MIND:
This experience hurts and feels uncomfortable, but I know I will find someone I like.

Reasonable Mind

Wise Mind

Emotional Mind

Consider when it would prove helpful to operate more in the logical mind. Perhaps when taking a test, making a major purchase, or studying. Likewise, when would it become important to allow ourselves to stay more in our emotional minds? Many situations involve appropriate moments to express and emote feelings, like at a funeral, making love, or writing poetry.

Reflect on the things that make you feel alive. From enjoying people and activities to values and beliefs that align with your life path, nurturing passion should create a trembling deep inside, shaking the soul alive. Passionate energy motivates, creates, and invigorates the mind into acting and moving forward.

Identifying our passion should involve a deeper look inward to inventory relationships or situations that no longer serve our highest good. This might mean changing and shifting away from people or environments that create stagnation or drain energy. Finding the holes that allow our spirits to become depleted and filling them with fuel instead can allow a little spark to reignite excitement in a passionless life. Passion energizes, electrifies, revitalizes, and baptizes the spirit, filling life with energy, meaning, and purpose.

❀ The Passion of Art ❀

Give examples of each type of art below
and how it reflects passion.

Literature ....

....

Visual arts ....

....

Theater/movies/TV series ....

....

Music ....

....

Shake My Soul

In this exercise, let's examine the areas in your life that dampen your energy, leaving you depleted or numb, while identifying the things that spark you to feel alive and energized.

Things, Situations, or People That...

Drain Me	Energize Me

Dull Me	Inspire Me

Bring Me Down	Uplift Me

Trap Me	Free Me

Demotivate Me	Motivate Me

WEEK
31

Peace in Frenzied Minds

Letting go gives us freedom, and freedom is the only condition for happiness. If, in our heart, we still cling to anything — anger, anxiety, or possessions — we cannot be free.

— THICH NHAT HANH, *The Heart of the Buddha's Teaching*

The Merriam-Webster dictionary defines nurturing as "to care for and encourage the growth or development of someone or something." Peace involves calm, tranquility, and freedom from chaotic disturbances. Nurturing peace, then, involves the care and growth of calmness.

One way to nurture peace in our lives comes from finding peace of mind. Letting go of guilt for past mistakes is a powerful way to connect with inner peace. This must involve releasing regret and guilt. Sometimes guilt and shame become intertwined, creating complications. Guilt comes from acting incongruently with our values, whereas shame comes from believing in our unworthiness. As a therapist, I see many people burdened with shame, which often leads to toxicity in their lives. Nothing good comes from shame. Shame-based beliefs often start with self-blame and a lack of compassion for

our situation and being human. Inner peace can evolve from self-forgiveness, gentleness, and extending grace to ourselves.

Consider for a moment what it would feel like to have peace in your heart even as things seem to fall apart around you. This peace would come from having moved through grief, struggles, or suffering with radical acceptance and letting go of unhelpful and hurtful thought patterns, behaviors, or people. Whether internalized or externalized and displaced onto another person or situation, shame-based beliefs feed angst and discontent. Worry thoughts, which spin around in our minds creating worst-case scenarios, drive fear-based reactions like paralyzing, freezing, or reacting with anger toward others, contributing to a sense of discord within and around us.

Nurturing peace involves self-reflection and awareness of these internal negative thoughts. The meaning given to a situation has the power to change everything. For instance, if I worry about breaking down on the side of the road, I might avoid driving or experience recurring panic and anxiety, which would cause challenges in my life.

Nurturing peace doesn't mean ignoring threats by sticking our heads in the sand or avoiding situations by becoming complacent with inaction. Nurturing peace means finding balance in meaning and perspective-shifting to tolerate or accept the moment when we're unable to change it. Peace comes from within regardless of what happens around us. It starts with our thoughts and the meaning placed on the events in our lives.

Boundaries, both internal and external, help foster peace. Protecting our energy and physical and emotional space fosters an ability to block unwanted

Release Shame by Changing Your Inner Narrative

Finding inner peace involves recognizing inner self-talk and creating a kinder, more forgiving tone. This does not mean releasing accountability for things that need to change. Rather, nurturing peace involves mindfully noticing without judgment and taking a step toward encouragement, whether making changes or accepting situations. Here are some negative self-talk statements that could use a little kindness or forgiveness in the name of internal peace. How do these examples show up in your life?

- I am a failure. I can't do anything right.
- No one likes me.
- I can't motivate myself. I'm so lazy.
- I'm such an idiot.
- I should have known better.

intrusions. Sometimes others can violate boundaries, imposing their own wishes or demands. When you're placating or allowing boundary violations, peace falls to the wayside. Resentment takes the wheel in its place, driving us into a further disconnect from our true self.

This chaos creates discord and noise as we become stretched thin and pulled in different directions. Frenzied running around from one event to the next in the endless pursuit of pleasing others creates imbalance and fosters exhaustion, a far cry from peace. In fact, in our society, keeping busy and productive has become a badge of worthiness earned through comparison and keeping up with those around us. It feels counterintuitive to relax and nurture peace when fighting for worthiness and approval, but it is essential.

Another angle to explore when finding ways to nurture peace involves looking into how external surroundings or situations and internal conflicts and judgments create imbalance. The news, advertising, and even social media sensationalize and elicit strong emotional responses by comparing to others, creating a fear of missing out or not being good enough, or encouraging a need for a constant stream of breaking stories. Meant to engage the viewer or listener for more views, followers, or purchases, these external peace robbers demand our energy through time, emotion, and money, creating imbalance and a pull away from our true self.

Helpful Hacks for Finding Peace

I've learned a few things about human nature in my career. Here's a quick-and-dirty list of some concepts I've come to realize might help when feeling overwhelmed.

- Most people consider how things impact themselves first.
- People don't change unless they want to.
- Limit exposure to social media or take a social media break. Detox from the news as needed.
- Find time alone or with those who create peace in your life.
- Engage in self-care strategies to nurture calmness in the mind and body like yoga, meditation, prayer, reading, or exercise.

Peace in My World
Reflection Questions

How can I set better boundaries in my life to protect my energy from becoming depleted or pulled in too many directions?

....

....

....

....

Who or what creates chaos in my life? How can I make changes to this?

....

....

....

....

Who or what situations nurture peace and calm in my world?
How can I find ways to increase this?

....

....

....

....

Describe or draw a situation that creates a feeling of calm and peace.

....

....

....

....

Nature in Modern Lives

*Live in each season as it passes; breathe the air,
drink the drink, taste the fruit, and
resign yourself to the influence of the earth.*

— HENRY DAVID THOREAU, *Walden*

One of the quickest and most powerful ways for me to become grounded and participate in nurturing myself involves surrounding myself in nature. My fondest memories from childhood involve exploring the world around me, from sledding and building snowmen to foraging in the great bamboo forest, making magic potions while crushing glittery rocks, and finding tiny flowers in my mom's flower beds. To this day, I find pleasure and peace outdoors.

Spending time in nature offers a simple, cheap, grounding, and beautiful way to decompress from modern life. Nurturing nature involves appreciating the elements of our world. While the periodic table lists 118 elements, the major elements like fire, water, air, metal, wood, and earth historically and cross-culturally carry meaning and universal associations. Each brings a component of life and has characteristics worth exploring.

- Fire evokes passion, force, and creativity
- Water evokes feelings, movement, healing, purification, and life force
- Air evokes intellect, communication, knowledge, and analysis
- Metal evokes alchemy, change, strength, and courage
- Wood evokes growth, life, and expansion
- Earth evokes nurturing, stability, generosity, and grounding

Reflecting on nature and how it impacts our lives brings an opportunity for introspection and connection to something greater than ourselves. Nothing feels more natural than spending time in the untainted world around us and relishing in the splendors of Mother Nature as she teaches us powerful lessons.

From seasonal, water, energy, plant, planetary, life, and even disease cycles, nature repeats and evolves in a constant flow around us. Let's look at some examples. With most of the earth's water held in oceans, fresh water is somewhat sparse. Yet, nature has a way of keeping water constant through evaporation, condensation, and precipitation. The sun, our perfectly distanced star responsible for life, allows for most energy sources in our world, outside of atomic energy. Plants, a foundation for ecosystems, use solar energy to make food from air, water, and minerals in the earth. Those plants and animals eventually die and return to the earth's soil, becoming packed down over millions of years, creating fossil fuels in many different forms — solid coal, liquid petroleum, and natural gases. Even our Milky Way galaxy cycles, revolving in a circle while the stars move around its center. The sun, earth, moon, and other planets each turn on their axes, and in turn they orbit around the sun or another body, changing daylight to darkness and days to years.

Nature teaches us balance and flow and adapting and accepting change, for everything starts, ends, and then begins again.

Spending time in nature allows for complete immersion and grounding

What Are Your Nature Faves?

- Water or land?
- Rain or sun?
- Mountains or beaches?
- Desert or forest?
- Clouds or grass?
- Moonlight or sunlight?
- Stars or sky?
- Plants or animals?
- Manicured or natural?
- Ocean or river?
- Flowers or greenery?
- Rocky cliffs or sand?
- Surfing or hiking?
- Skiing or tubing?

into a world filled with beauty and inspiration. Nurturing nature becomes a way to nurture ourselves, as we too play a role in the natural world. From tapping into our full sensory experiences with mindfulness to relishing the fresh air, beautiful scenery, and simple escape from man-made influences, nature creates a space and moment of respite and renewal. Nothing speaks more to the soul than the pristine, untouched, and natural world. Nature reminds us that we exist as part of something greater.

Mindfully spending time in nature involves fully tuning in to the entire range of sensory experiences. As discussed in previous chapters, the quickest and sometimes easiest way to practice mindfulness involves tuning in to our five senses and observing and noticing those experiences in the moment. With focused stillness, a sense of freedom and escape from our busy minds and man-made lives allows for connection and grounding to our world and life source.

Whether nature brings you closer to spiritually connecting with a creator or whether you enjoy the scientific aspects of nature, the simple complexity and reflection of meaning create lessons worth noting. Every living thing must change and end. Energy can neither be created nor destroyed, thus instead working itself through cycles and changes. Systems work together to support growth and change. Nature defies human power and influence as storms, natural disasters, and natural wonders that continue to shock, awe, and amaze us with their impact. Nature is truly a force to respect and appreciate.

Nature Hunt

For this activity, spend at least ten minutes in nature and tune in to your senses. Find a small treasure or token during this time, perhaps a leaf, shell, or small flower. Practice mindfully observing this gift from nature as you become more appreciative of the world around you.

Afterward, reflect on the experience. What did you notice? What was your sensory experience like? How did this inspire you? What did you learn and take away from this time in nature?

Nurturing Nature

What are your favorite ways to spend time in nature?
Fill in the petals with your answers.

WEEK

33

Nourishment for Our Bodies

Call a truce, stop the food fight! Give yourself unconditional permission to eat. If you tell yourself that you can't or shouldn't have a particular food, it can lead to intense feelings of deprivation that build into uncontrollable cravings and, often, bingeing.

— EVELYN TRIBOLE AND ELYSE RESCH, *Intuitive Eating*

Nurturing our bodies is essential for sustaining life. Like a vehicle, our bodies need food and maintenance to fuel us through the ups and downs of life. This chapter focuses on the experience of nourishing our bodies and what it means, not judgment or debate about healthy versus unhealthy foods or lifestyle choices, which can be found in many other sources outside this book.

Food obviously offers nourishment in a physical sense; certain nutrients like vitamins and minerals, fat, and protein allow our cells to grow and repair, helping our bodies function optimally. But sometimes food provides emotional comfort too. It helps to know the difference between physical and emotional hunger. The former slowly evolves and grows and is eventually satiated with any food choice. For example, in the morning you may notice a slight twitch of hunger that intensifies by lunchtime. This physical hunger is slower, growing, and easily remedied.

Emotional hunger, though, comes on more quickly, with urgency, and often with specific cravings in response to a sometimes known, and other times subconscious, emotional trigger. Picture coming home after a stressful day of work to find yourself immediately looking in the freezer for ice cream. Before even realizing it, you're eating a gallon of the stuff. While some might see this as nurturing, eating in this way could provide numbing and avoidance for stressful emotions. This attempt to self-soothe can develop into a pattern often found in disordered emotional eating or eating disorders like bulimia or binge-eating disorder.

Modern life allows us the luxury to enjoy food outside of survival purposes alone. Because of this, it has become influenced by human judgment as something to control, fear, and judge as good or bad. Beyond the natural need for nourishment, economic considerations like the agricultural or livestock industry, the diet and health industry, and the beauty and fashion industry all drive beliefs about food. Plagued with sugar, caloric, and carbohydrate counts, food has become laced with judgment. Nourishing our bodies might mean eating cleaner foods, more naturally grown and harvested, and perhaps allowing a variety of nutrient-dense foods while delighting in the pleasure and enjoyment of tasting sweet and savory flavors. Balance is key in creating a healthy relationship with food and discerning the influence of advertising, propaganda, and economic-driven marketing.

As a therapist working with eating disorders, I have seen food and body image distorted by advertising and the influence of our societal norms, which fluctuate over time. There have been fat-free crazes, meat and dairy periods, low-carb and sugar-free phases, and gluten-free movements. I have also observed the changes in advertising. Just the other day, I noticed a popular, common, grain-based cereal with the words "plant-based" on the packaging. Two decades ago, the same product advertised itself as "fat-free."

On the positive side, food, with its sights, smells, and tastes, can also evoke strong images of warmth, comfort, and often nostalgia. My most cherished childhood memories center around family gatherings where food nourished our bodies, hearts, and souls. Passed down through generations, family recipes from both Kentucky and

There's No Good or Bad Food!

Think about the ways you conceptualize good versus bad food. Does this differ from five years ago, ten years ago, twenty years ago, or when you were a child? Consider how you can find more neutral ways to think about food.

Pennsylvania Dutch origins played a huge component in my life. The smell of biscuits and gravy and bacon and coffee in the mornings reminds me of the love and safety I felt as a child. My father cooking steak, ribs with his special sauce, and homemade pizza while my mom cooked the traditional Sunday meatloaf and mashed potatoes filled my heart with warmth and my belly with a rumble.

Perhaps you're like me, where food played a key role in how your family provided love and nurturing. Mealtime with loved ones offers an opportunity for connection, security, comfort, and rituals. I hope to pass along those family recipes and instill a sense of love through food as it nourishes and fills our bodies and hearts.

❀ Favorite Foods ❀

Use the prompts below to list foods that have a special place or impact on your life.

A favorite meal growing up: ....

....

Favorite comfort food when you are sick: ....

....

Favorite food to eat out: ....

....

Favorite food to eat at home: ....

....

Favorite cultural dish: ....

....

Favorite new dish (not eaten in childhood): ....

....

Food Is Love Inventory

YES	NO	
○	○	Food played a big part in my family in a positive way.
○	○	I received conflicting views about food from my family and society.
○	○	I use food as comfort when stressed, hurt, upset, angry, happy, and/or bored.
○	○	I restrict my food intake for non-cosmetic health reasons (for example, diabetes, celiac disease, allergies).
○	○	I restrict my food to lose weight.
○	○	I believe there are good and bad foods.
○	○	I eat a variety of foods.
○	○	My comfort foods are sweets and carbs.
○	○	I believe food is fuel.
○	○	Food is pleasurable and makes me happy.
○	○	I often feel guilty when eating certain foods.
○	○	I believe my food choices negatively affect my appearance.
○	○	I look forward to eating meals.
○	○	I avoid eating out for health reasons.
○	○	I do not like eating in front of others.

Body Movement for Still Bodies

An early-morning walk is a blessing for the whole day.
— HENRY DAVID THOREAU, *Journals (1838–1859)*

Most of us enjoyed physical activity when we were kids, even if as adults it has lost its easy allure. For many of us, it's time to reconceptualize exercise from a have-to chore to something that feels good and sounds fun.

This shift away from spending hours in a stinky gym with fluorescent lights and a "How many calories am I burning?" mindset creates opportunities to move your body in more pleasing ways and environments. This isn't to say that working out in a gym is the wrong way to exercise, but rather that nurturing movement in our bodies can come from a place that offers freedom in expression and enjoyment in the process.

Imagine nurturing your body through movement for the simple enjoyment and amazement of how your body moves or how wonderful it feels. Releasing the all-consuming motivation to exercise solely for burning calories, being good, permission to eat something, or to look skinnier allows for freedom in movement to align with something greater.

For me, I chose to replace those old shame-driven motivators with the simple appreciation and joy of moving my body in ways that align with my natural athleticism, love for being outside, and maybe a little nostalgia thrown in the mix. Reflecting on your values can help you zero in on how to move your body.

In what ways does your moving body amaze, inspire, and delight you? Whether learning a new yoga pose, reaching a personal best for your first 5K, or catching a Frisbee®, moving our bodies sometimes sparks the desire to push ourselves beyond what we believed possible. Our bodies can do amazing things like bend, jump, kick, punch, stretch, flex, move, lift, and even chew, blink, and breathe. When facing barriers to movement from illness or conditions, we can still find joy in simple movements like yawning and stretching, bathing, or moving our heads to music.

How we come to enjoy movement depends partially on our own individualized and unique body's capabilities and how we choose to honor opportunities to move. Everyone will find their unique way to nurture movement. The key is making this enjoyable through gratitude, appreciation, and connecting with our true selves.

I recently realigned my values with nurturing authenticity and chose to reflect this through body movement. As a naturally athletic person, I became tired of only pushing myself to work out to lose weight or for health purposes, which contributed to shame-based beliefs of not being good enough. Instead, I have found ways to incorporate movement in a way that aligns with my authentic self. Playing volleyball with my kids, throwing a football, riding my bike, swimming, and walking on the beach become want-tos filled with enjoyment, friendly competition, and fun rather than drudgery and dread. You can learn to develop these want-tos too.

Think for a moment about how you enjoyed moving your body as a child. Perhaps you enjoyed sports or

Tips for Nurturing Movement for Enjoyment

Consider these three tips for creating a more meaningful and pleasurable exercise routine.

1. Your inner child must agree and want to join in! Find things you used to enjoy as a child. A little nostalgia goes a long way!

2. Do not find motivation in external goals like losing weight, looking better, being in good shape, lifting the heaviest weights, time spent, miles walked, or higher levels on the elliptical.

3. Align exercise with enjoyable sensory experiences. Connect with nature if that inspires you. Take a walk in the woods, on the beach, or even in the rain!

competitive games, or maybe you preferred to go for nature walks or ride your bike. Connecting with our inner child and ways that we found moving our bodies fun when we were young offers a chance to connect and honor our true inner self.

If nurturing movement feels impossible to incorporate into your daily routine, think for a moment about what internal and external barriers are preventing it. Perhaps these include time constraints, decreased energy or motivation, the weather, health issues, or finances. Reflect on these barriers and consider if there are underlying reasons for them that point toward not prioritizing movement. Consider things like self-sabotaging, feeling unworthy, or shame about not being good enough. I have heard some people say they can't move their body in certain ways they might enjoy because they are not thin enough. I have also heard others share that they don't have time, possibly due to not setting effective boundaries and over-functioning or prioritizing others over themselves.

As a working mother with sports-playing children, at some point working out became almost impossible for me to accommodate in my schedule. Eventually, I became resentful; I needed to readjust my expectations and consider taking a walk at practice or doing some stretching during lunch. Movement doesn't have to last hours and hours and involve tons of sweat to prove valuable. Every little moment and little way our bodies move offers benefits and appreciation.

Creative, Playful Ways to Move Your Body

- Dance in the kitchen when cooking dinner
- Leap around in a bouncy castle or trampoline
- Play dodgeball (use soft balls!)
- Jump rope and double Dutch
- Skip to music outside
- Go to a roller-skating rink (or in-line skate outside)
- Build a snowman or a sand mermaid
- Play freeze tag
- Blow up a balloon and don't let it touch the ground
- Pretend the floor is hot lava

Body Movement Calendar Challenge

Try to move your body in different ways every day and keep a log of your experience. You can even record movement that doesn't seem like exercise, like walking the dog, changing your bedsheets, or doing dishes.

	Type of movement	How I felt before	How I felt after	Enjoyment rating (0–10)
Sunday				
Monday				
Tuesday				
Wednesday				
Thursday				
Friday				
Saturday				

WEEK
35

Friendships in Lonely Hearts

*When we honestly ask ourselves which people
in our lives mean the most to us, we often find it is those who,
instead of giving advice, solutions, or cures, have chosen
instead to share our pain and touch our wounds
with a warm and tender hand.*

— HENRI J.M. NOUWEN, *Out of Solitude*

Have you ever felt lucky to have a best friend, a special person who loves and accepts you completely? Friendships have the power to shape us and transform our lives, allowing us to reach beyond our families to make connections in the world. Friends offer stability when life throws a curveball, support during difficult or painful times, and celebration for those fun and exciting moments in life.

As social beings, humans require connections with other humans, and friendships offer this companionship by fostering a sense of belonging. Having a loyal friend helps us feel safe, protected, and connected in creating a meaningful life worth living.

In 2009, a Dutch study by Gerald Mollenhorst[17] found that most friendships last about seven years. If a friendship remains intact beyond this, the chances it will last a lifetime increase. Most friendships come from opportunities with shared experiences to connect, as seen in school-aged children where the students in your class most often influence who becomes a friend. This makes sense, as most friendships require attention and time together for growth. If you're lucky, some special strongly bonded friendships allow for years to pass with little contact, only to pick right up where you left off when reconnecting. It's an unconditional love that withstands time and distance.

The Mayo Clinic has found that friendships can impact our health and well-being by reducing stress, improving confidence, and offering support through life changes. Studies show that those with adult friendships exhibit a reduced risk of depression, high blood pressure, and obesity. Older adults with meaningful connections tend to live longer than their lonely counterparts.[18]

Friendships come in all forms and degrees with no right or wrong in quantity or type. But while quantity might not matter, quality certainly does. In counseling middle school– and high school–age teenagers, I sometimes ask them to consider the traits they believe make a quality friend. During this developmental stage, teenagers will begin to separate themselves from their families, leaning more toward their peer connections as they develop autonomy and identity. Choosing quality

friendships involves trust, effective and open communication, respect, inclusion, and reciprocity. Without these aspects, a friendship might become imbalanced over time, with one person giving more than they receive, leading to codependency or toxicity.

Think about your favorite friend and what qualities make this person special to you. Consider how those qualities become important in a relationship. Recognizing when to let go of a friendship that no longer offers support, respect, or reciprocity is essential for allowing space for new or healthier relationships to emerge. Consider giving energy only to those relationships and connections that nourish the soul, share alignment with values, and enrich life, allowing inauthentic, competitive, or superficial relationships to fade away.

For those with more introverted tendencies, social anxiety, or life

Friendship Analysis

Think about friendships you have. What qualities do you look for in a friendship, from the following list or otherwise?

- Loyalty
- Shared values
- Similar interests
- Kindness

- Effective communication
- Humor
- Fun
- Acceptance

changes requiring the need to form new connections, the idea of making new friends might create anxiety and bring up insecurities. I sometimes wish making adult friends was as simple as it was in kindergarten: "You're wearing a yellow shirt. Yellow is my favorite color. Let's be best friends."

Forming friendships in adulthood can prove challenging, as the opportunities to connect decrease. In school, surrounded by others your age, more opportunities existed, even if it didn't seem that way at the time. For many adults, friendships form through work, children, shared interests, and even social media. As we grow and evolve, our circle can widen for potential friendships that offer more richness and diversity, expanding beyond similar ages, environments, or backgrounds.

What do you find challenging about making friends as an adult? What has worked for you in terms of organic opportunities? In what ways do you struggle to find connections or initiate making friends? Have you considered more direct ways to create an opportunity for connection? Exploring these questions might help troubleshoot feelings of loneliness and disconnection. Nurturing new and old friendships requires an intentional investment of effort, time, and energy. Lasting friendships do not happen magically, though it can feel magical when that special connection and acceptance happens.

Ways to Make Friends as an Adult

- Join a site for shared interests, such as Meet Me
- Take a class (belly dancing, reiki)
- Join a book club
- Participate in religious groups or services
- Volunteer
- Invite a colleague to lunch or a movie
- Walk your pet outside
- Strike up a conversation with a stranger
- Try an app for matching with friends, such as Bumble

Friend-ventory,

Fill in the faces with people in your world whom
you consider friends as well as each of the other categories.

Stranger
(potential friend)

Friend of
a friend

Acquaintance/
colleague

Friend

Inner circle

The Spotlight for Our Inner Wallflower

*The secret to life is to put yourself in the right lighting.
For some, it's a Broadway spotlight; for others, a lamplit desk.
Use your natural powers — of persistence, concentration,
and insight — to do work you love and work that matters.
Solve problems, make art, think deeply.*

— SUSAN CAIN, *Quiet*

How do you show up in the world? Do you enjoy the limelight and center stage? Or, like me, do you prefer to hide behind the scenes? Some of this preference for how to show up might stem from insecurities, societal or familial conditioning, or personality type. When self-doubt kicks in, feelings of discomfort and vulnerability step to the front, urging us to hide or diminish our light. Imagine how many people stay in the shadows who have a wonderful gift, talent, or message to share in the world.

After I wrote my first book, *Self-Love Workbook for Women,* new opportunities to share and connect with others emerged. Several podcast shows invited me on as a guest. Up to this point, I had always hidden behind closed doors and the four walls of my counseling office, working one-on-one with clients. The idea of speaking in front of people to share with larger groups felt scary. Luckily, my passion for my mission to help women love themselves allowed me to push beyond this fear. I allowed myself to expand beyond my comfort zone to shine my light and message to others in new ways.

One way to show up in our media-heavy and virtually connected world involves photographs. Those who engage with social media tend to enjoy quick glimpses offered by images and videos. Posting a picture puts you out there in the world. This isn't to say that you need to post photos of yourself — but consider opening yourself up to the experience of a personal photo shoot.

I recently enjoyed a photo shoot with photographer Debbie Smith with FiftyLove Photography, who specializes in photo shoots for women over forty. Debbie taught me that hiding myself in the shadows did not align with my message and mission. I realized I couldn't help other women embrace themselves if I didn't let go of my own fears and self-doubt. Our photo shoot filled me with confidence, laughter, and fun; it was almost therapeutically empowering. I walked away from my experience feeling truly beautiful, realizing my worth comes not from my physical appearance but my inner magic captured on camera. With the help of a professional photographer, a passionate friend, or even your own skills, consider having a similar photo shoot to unlock your personal light.

Photo Shoot Reflection

How do you feel about being in the spotlight or showing up in the world? ....

....

....

Have you ever had a photo shoot experience? If so, what was it like? If not, what holds you back? ....

....

....

How do you feel about being in pictures and having them posted on social media? ....

....

....

Another component to stepping into the spotlight involves knowing our gifts and understanding how to share them in the world. While not everyone needs to stay in the spotlight, we all have gifts to share. Wallflowers, often standing and watching from the sidelines, may hold back in sharing their gifts through anxiety, fear of embarrassment, or a more introverted personality type. Nurturing the spotlight involves nurturing confidence and empowerment to share and show up in the world.

Introverts often feel pressure to show up in more socially engaging ways than what feels natural. But nurturing the spotlight does not mean changing personality types or doing something that feels unnatural. It means finding ways to show up in the world authentically and share your gifts. This may happen behind the scenes, like in a theater production. Stage and technical crew work in the shadows with costumes, props, lighting, sound, and set design while the actors take center stage. Everyone involved plays a crucial role in the production, deserving appreciation, recognition, and acknowledgment on the stage. Knowing which role feels most comfortable to you helps you determine how to show up in the world.

Behind the Scenes or Spotlight Quiz

YES	NO	
○	○	I prefer to be publicly recognized for my contributions.
○	○	I feel comfortable having my picture taken and shared on social media.
○	○	I know my gifts and strengths.
○	○	I feel self-conscious when others notice me.
○	○	I prefer to work unnoticed behind the scenes.
○	○	People in the spotlight are attention seekers.
○	○	Those behind the scenes are insecure and shy.

Step into the Spotlight

Fill in the stage with personality traits, qualities, strengths, talents, or messages you can share in the world. In the curtains, fill in your fears and insecurities that keep you hidden in the shadows.

Our Lives through Our Five Senses

I think the real miracle is not to walk either on water or in thin air, but to walk on earth. Every day we are engaged in a miracle which we don't even recognize: a blue sky, white clouds, green leaves, the black, curious eyes of a child — our own two eyes. All is a miracle.

— THICH NHAT HANH, *The Miracle of Mindfulness*

By this point in the book, you should have a strong awareness of mindfulness and how to apply it in your life. A quick, engaging way to practice building the mindfulness muscle involves tuning in to the full sensory experience.

Our human brain uses the five senses to gather and process information instantly about the world around us, allowing for safety and survival. Sensory experiences offer enjoyment and connect us instantly to our brain's emotional and memory parts. The five major senses of sight, sound, taste, smell, and touch work together to gather information to detect threats in our surroundings. Another form of sensory input, our vestibular system, also provides information on balance and body positioning. Let's explore each of the five major senses in more depth and the importance of nurturing them.

Touch: Offers protection by noticing pain with temperature differences, textures for testing food for ripeness or decay, and an important social connection with others needed for survival.

Sight: A dominant sense that helps us navigate the world by identifying threats, finding food, and communicating with others. Vision helps us to move and balance our body positions.

Smell: Important for identifying safe and edible food sources. Smell is directly linked to memory centers in the brain. Pheromones influence attraction for procreation.

Taste: Linked to smell and food choices. Taste buds offer important information for different dietary needs and survival.

Sound: Important for communication and learning. Hearing potential threats in the environment helps with survival.

While our senses allow our survival, they also offer pleasure and enjoyment and a way of fueling connecting to others and the world around us. Learning to practice mindfulness through observing and noticing sensations requires intentional practice and pulling away from distractions. Mindful awareness allows for connection and grounding into our bodies. Our sensory input is a tangible way to refocus and bring our attention back to the current moment and what our bodies experience.

My Senses

Which of the five senses do you appreciate or enjoy the most?

....

....

....

If you had to give up one sense, which would you choose?

....

....

Do you have any limitations with your sensory experience?
Describe what this is like for you.

....

....

....

Nurturing our senses means being present and aware; it is the opposite of dissociation and disconnection. Daydreaming, numbing, and distracting behaviors like zoning out or becoming immersed in a book or binge-watching a series pull us away from body and sensory experiences.

I recently experienced my first live crystal bowl sound bath at the beach after doing yoga. A sound bath is an experience where someone rubs or taps mallets along the outside of a crystal bowl to create beautiful sounds and vibrations of all frequencies. Loud and harmonious, the sounds reverberate on a cellular level; I could feel them down to the core of my body. This experience inspired me to purchase my own crystal bowls and take a course in the practice! If you haven't experienced a sound bath, I highly recommend it. This experience exemplifies what nurturing just one of the senses might feel like. Consider the different ways your senses come to life and create full engagement with the world around you.

Benefits to Sound Baths

If you cannot go to a live sound bath, consider listening to one on YouTube.

- Promotes relaxation and a deeper sense of peace
- Improves sleep
- Rejuvenates and recharges
- Lowers stress and anxiety
- Improves mood
- Increases energy and focus
- Deepens state of consciousness and awareness
- Encourages mindfulness and grounding in the present
- Reduces depression
- Lowers blood pressure and slows breathing patterns, like meditation does

NOTE: Before participating in a live sound bath, please consider checking with your medical provider if you are pregnant, allergic to metals, or have metal plates, pacemakers, or other conditions like migraines or epilepsy that might cause sensitivity to sound and vibrations.

Nurturing the Five Senses

In the space below, share an experience in which you
practice mindfulness and focus using each sense. Consider ways
in the future that you can nurture this sense.

Sight

Smell

Taste

Touch

Hearing

Playfulness in Serious Minds

Play is often talked about as if it were a relief from serious learning. But for children, play IS serious learning. At various times, play is a way to cope with life and to prepare for adulthood. Playing is a way to solve problems and to express feelings. In fact, play is the real work of childhood.

— FRED ROGERS

Nothing feels more delightful than watching a child frolic and play, singing, dancing, and squealing in delight. Children have an enviable sense of wonder and a reckless abandon that allow for freedom in expression and creativity. Nurturing playfulness in adults must involve suspending judgment, criticism, constraints, and control. The freedom that comes with playfulness creates opportunities to awaken and engage the world fully.

Playfulness feels light and fun, though the work of play brings about heavy benefits. Play allows for stress-relieving, endorphin-stimulating, creativity-fueled inspiration and connection, opening the windows to air out our stuffy lives filled with responsibility and endless to-do lists.

Understanding the different types of play helps identify a child's developmental and therapeutic needs. For adults, understanding the different types of

play offers a chance to pinpoint exactly what seems to be missing in life and find ways to fill the gaps. Child development experts identify six to eleven types of play important for child development. It makes sense that adults explore these too, for we once were children.

Let's take a deeper look into some of these and how they might show up in nurturing play in an adult world.

Parallel play: Beginning around age two, children sit around other children while each child plays separately and independently. During this time, they become aware of each other, observe, and may mimic different play choices.

Dramatic/imaginative play: Young children ages four to eight enjoy dramatic, imaginative play through make-believe and dress-up with role-playing. This play is often highly imaginative and fantasy-based, with themes of good guys versus bad guys and heroes and heroines. Conflicts, validation, and empathy can be seen in this play, as well as cooperation, taking turns, and inclusivity.

Symbolic play: Children begin to express themselves through art by drawing, painting, working with clay, rhyming through music, and singing. This creative expression allows them to process emotions in a full sensory manner.

Constructive play: This play involves building and creating things like sandcastles, pillow forts, and building block structures. It requires trial and error to figure out how to make something stand up, and perseverance to keep trying.

Cooperative play: This play stage happens around preschool, ages four and five, and continues throughout childhood. Cooperative play involves inviting others and playing with others through board games, group activities, or joining forces to create.

Competitive play: Playing board games or other games like tag or sports while following rules and dealing with winning and losing. This play requires emotional regulation and dealing with losing and good sportsmanship.

Physical play: Engaging the body in movement using fine and gross motor skills. This play often involves balls, jump ropes, climbing, running, or riding a bike.

Consider the ways play seems indulgent or impossible in your life. What preconceptions or misconceptions do you have about play? Often, adults feel childish or that they are too mature for play or simplistic concepts. Perhaps it feels uncomfortable to lose control or to make a mess. Some adults do not enjoy competition, preferring more cooperative or symbolic forms of play.

Take a moment to consider the barriers to incorporating play into your life. As a mother, I found ways to incorporate play by engaging my kids in playful experiences like game night, painting activities, and four-square competitions on the beach. In play therapy sessions, I have the privilege to become invited into dramatic play. Here are some myths about play worth debunking if you find yourself resisting play:

1. **It's too messy:** The freedom to make a mess feels liberating and offers a chance to go outside the norm. Messier forms of play also offer a multisensory experience.

2. **It's too childish:** While play has important developmental milestones for children, it can continue to last into adulthood, as play forms the foundation for building qualities important in life like creativity, problem-solving, imagination, cooperation, and emotional regulation. I know a few adults who could benefit from further development in these areas.

3. **I don't have time to play:** The benefits of play call for making space in life for it. Perhaps finding a balance between the have-tos and the want-tos makes sense.

Playtime!

Consider different ways to incorporate play into your adult life.

1. Have a board game night
2. Play dodgeball or volleyball
3. Go boogie boarding or sledding
4. Build a snowman or a sandcastle
5. Paint, color, create
6. Move your body in fun ways
7. Laugh loudly
8. Dance in the rain
9. Pick flowers
10. Sing in the car or try karaoke

Ideas for Play

Let's look at the different kinds of play (described earlier) and how they might show up in your life. Add other examples to the ones I've provided. Consider choosing at least one day a month to incorporate play into your life.

PARALLEL PLAY:

Sitting next to a friend while you both play a video game

DRAMATIC PLAY:

Role-playing at a murder mystery party

SYMBOLIC PLAY:

Decorating a gingerbread house

CONSTRUCTIVE PLAY:

Building with Lego®

COOPERATIVE PLAY:

Building a sandcastle together

COMPETITIVE PLAY:

Playing a board game

PHYSICAL PLAY:

Playing volleyball

SUMMER

★ WEEK ★

39

Uniqueness in a Copy and Paste World

*We are sun and moon, dear friend; we are sea and land.
It is not our purpose to become each other; it is to recognize
each other, to learn to see the other and honor him for what he is:
each the other's opposite and complement.*

— HERMANN HESSE, *Narcissus and Goldmund*

Think back to middle school, when most kids simply want to fit in with others. Preteens often become cookie-cutter imitations, copying the latest trends and fads. Most of us grow out of this behavior. Some even full-on reject it by going completely against the grain. Eventually, most adults evolve to the point of knowing themselves and finding their own identity and uniqueness.

With social media playing a large role in our lives, staying authentic and nurturing our uniqueness can feel intimidating, given the urge to compare and keep up. Standing out might feel vulnerable or trigger feelings from earlier life experiences of being left out or made fun of for being different. Learning to nurture our uniqueness involves finding the courage to stand out and embrace our whole self. Think how boring the world would be if no one nurtured their unique qualities. No one has lived your life and shared your exact perspectives and experiences.

What qualities or experiences make you special? Perhaps you have experienced or overcome something not many have encountered, or perhaps you have a unique way of thinking about the world. The natural neurodiversity of the human brain, combined with owning our individual story, creates a cause for celebration rather than copying and pasting to be like someone else.

Growing up, my parents identified and nurtured my sisters' and my own special strengths and talents. As kids, we clung to this specialness as part of our identity, not realizing we could also be good at other things. My smart, organized sister now enjoys triathlons. My musically talented sister earned her MBA, CPA, and now her master of divinity. Athletic Megan excelled academically in college and went on to write and publish two books. I share this to help explain that while we all have special qualities, this should not box us in or limit us in any way.

Now, you might be thinking you have nothing that makes you special. But everyone has a uniqueness that sets them apart from others. It doesn't have to be specialized talents or qualities, but perhaps your experiences, life story, or family heritage. Spending time to determine how you show up in the world helps foster diversity and makes the world more beautiful and complex. Imagine if all humans experienced

❀ Unique Me ❀

Identify something unique about you. ....

....

....

How did you develop this awareness? ....

....

....

Who played a role in helping you realize your special qualities?

....

....

the same lives, stories, experiences, thoughts, and feelings.

Personality tests like the Myers-Briggs Personality Inventory (MBPI) or the Enneagram offer an organized description of personality types. Yet even within these types, diversity and uniqueness happen, as no one shares the same experience and story. The traits and characteristics described in these tests can provide eye-opening information and help validate how you deal with conflict or source your energy in social situations. While informative and entertaining, these tests fall short of identifying your uniqueness. I know several people in my family who share the same MBPI type (as it happens, INFJ). Nevertheless, our unique perspectives and qualities show up in different ways, making us all very different.

When exploring unique qualities, consider personality traits like humor, special interests, creativity, talents, physical characteristics, life experiences, family, and cultural backgrounds — all of these play a part in your story. What values drive you and are important in your life? How does this differ from those around you in your workplace, home, friends, or family?

❀ Interview with Others ❀

Ask someone you know to share why they think you are unique. It might surprise you how others see you and pick up on qualities you might not know you have. How is this different or the same as how you see yourself?

....

....

....

....

....

....

The Me Tree

Fill out this page with the things that, together, make you uniquely you.

Likes, interests, and qualities
(leaves)

Areas to grow and expand
(branches)

Core values and beliefs
(trunk)

WEEK
40

Gratitude in Grumpy Hearts

Gratitude makes sense of our past, brings peace for today, and creates a vision for tomorrow.

— MELODIE BEATTIE, *The Language of Letting Go*

This might be my favorite chapter, for I once lived in pessimist land and escaped by way of gratitude. Perpetually finding the negative and preparing for the worst, I lamented in situations, attaching meaning, creating unnecessary misery and suffering. I sometimes had a hard time improving negative moments in my life due to some pesky stinky thinking. This led to a frequently grumpy and irritable version of myself.

During my childhood, every summer, my family spent a week at the beach. Often in the morning, my sisters and I would complain about the fog, fearing the cloudy, wet weather would last all day, making the beach trip a bust. My father, always the perpetual optimist, would say with ninety-percent accuracy, "Don't worry, the fog will burn off." Instead of thinking negatively and creating a moment of frustration, his positive thinking offered hope and a chance to wait and see. This neutral to positive way of thinking can help alleviate negative moods and improve dynamics and relationships with those around us.

Thinking about something that makes us feel upset and learning to defuse through neutral to positive thoughts helps improve the moment. At times, gratitude allows for thankfulness when reflecting on others who might have it worse off. This isn't meant to invalidate challenges and difficulties, but rather to foster appreciation through perspective-shifting.

So, what does it mean to practice gratitude, and how do you do it? The first step in practicing gratitude involves acknowledging the current situation, even when difficult or uncomfortable.

When suppressing or disconnecting from uncomfortable feelings, practicing gratitude devolves into a superficial attempt to put a bandage over a gaping wound or sweep something under the rug. Allowing "positive vibes only" encourages a potentially toxic approach to artificially creating more comfortable emotions, missing the point of gratitude. Finding small ways to appreciate situations, even uncomfortable ones, allows true gratitude to shine through.

The balance of validating uncomfortable emotions or situations with gratitude looks and sounds like mindfulness.

Observing and noticing the uncomfortable without judgment creates an opportunity to add thanks for something in that moment. Perhaps you are stuck in a traffic jam due to an accident and stressed about a late arrival. A quick gratitude check might include thinking about the poor individuals involved in the accident and expressing thanks for not being involved in the wreck. This doesn't overshadow the concerns of being late, but instead keeps them in perspective with things that could be worse.

Grrr-attitude Adjustment

Give the following negative comments an attitude adjustment.

Grumpy Thought	Bright Side
Kids these days…	I was a kid once too.
It's freezing cold. I hate snow.	
She's so annoying.	
I don't feel like working today.	
People are idiots.	

It's worth looking deeper into toxic positivity when exploring gratitude. Have you ever felt dismissed or discounted by someone attempting to make you feel better with a comment like "Just think positively" or "Look on the bright side"? While these sentiments might prove helpful or ring true in theory, if they are said at the wrong time, in the wrong way, or by the wrong person, they can come off as invalidating, patronizing, or flat-out annoying. Often, toxic positivity comes from a place of discomfort and an attempt to cover up or fix suffering or pain.

As a therapist, I have learned the subtle art of knowing when to validate and allow venting and when to shift to a more helpful perspective. When a client says, "Yeah, but" or keeps presenting barriers or obstacles to something I suggest, that offers a clue to when I should stop talking and just listen. Providing empathy involves connecting with the uncomfortable, not using overly positive platitudes that simplify the complexity of the sharer's emotions and situation. Eventually, skills, suggestions, challenges, and perspective-shifting can happen — but only in the context of first being seen, heard, and understood.

Toxic Positivity versus Gratitude

Toxic Positivity	Gratitude
Uncomfortable with negative emotions	Allows acceptance of reality
Falsely reassures	Notices and observes
Drives disconnection	Creates connection
Too simplistic	Holds complexity in a simple way
Common phrases	Unique to situation
Suppression of feelings	Acknowledgment of feelings

Seven-Day Gratitude Challenge

For this exercise, consider participating in a Seven-Day
Gratitude Challenge by recording what you are grateful for each day.

Sunday

Monday

Tuesday

Wednesday

Thursday

Friday

Saturday

At the end of the week, share about a time when you transformed
your negative, grumpy attitude into a more grateful mindset.

Diversity in Boring Lives

It is time for parents to teach young people early on that in diversity there is beauty and there is strength.

— MAYA ANGELOU

As shared in a previous chapter, I recently had the vulnerable experience of going to a nude beach. It was exhilarating, but, more importantly, the experience allowed me to appreciate the diversity in our bodies. I saw different shapes, sizes, skin, and hair colors. My nakedness wasn't what stood out to me the most; instead, what stood out was how different and boring the experience would have felt if every body on the beach looked the same.

Diversity comes in many shapes and forms, from our body's different capabilities and the neurodiversity of our brains to our culture, language, race, spiritual beliefs, gender, sexuality, faith, and political affiliations. How truly boring it would be if humans were all the same. Surrounding ourselves with those who look, act, or believe the same way as we do allows for a loss of variety and richness from experiencing different perspectives. Nurturing diversity involves growing appreciation and comfort for those differences and interactions with others and the world around us. This requires a willingness to have an open mind, embrace change, and overcome fear and discomfort.

Diversity calls for expansion beyond our narrow mindset and a shift toward appreciating differences with respect and celebration. Humans tend to gravitate toward people or situations that feel similar and familiar, reducing the likelihood of finding comfort in embracing differences. An appreciation of diversity can come from more exposure and education.

A helpful framework to conceptualize diversity involves categorizing how it shows up in the world in both internal, inherent traits as well as in external aspects. Internal traits and characteristics begin at birth and include race, ethnicity, age, sex, physical and cognitive abilities, and neurodiversity. External experiences like education, workplace, geography, finances, and living situations are more mutable and add to life's diversity spectrum. Humans also tend to form bonds with those with similar interests, likes, and worldviews, including faith-based or politically-based belief systems, creating yet another layer. The power of diversity comes from recognizing and appreciating the human complexity within the world.

One important component to appreciating differences is an openness to stop and listen. By seeking to understand and listen to those who differ from us, growth, learning, and new perspectives emerge, fostering more creativity, depth, and awareness. Through tuning into the differences rather than rejecting or dismissing them, a new appreciation and respect can surface, allowing for deeper understanding and richness. Imagine

Diversity Check

Consider for a moment the earliest time you recognized differences in others. Perhaps it was age, gender, skin color, or language. Reflect on the significance of this awareness and how it helped shape your view of diversity.

....

....

....

....

....

....

eating a salad that only consisted of lettuce. The salad becomes more enjoyable with different textures, colors, and flavors from other vegetables, croutons, nuts, or dressing.

A lack of diversity often shows up in the form of biases and judgments toward situations or people. This perpetuates an "us versus them" mentality, adding to fear and prejudice. While some might believe that seeing no differences encourages equality, the acceptance and even appreciation of differences lead to a richer and more complete picture of embracing diversity. The beauty comes from the differences themselves, not from ignoring them or pretending they don't exist.

Often bias and judgments happen subconsciously. Because of this, nurturing diversity must involve self-awareness and honest conversations outside our comfort levels about differences while recognizing where our beliefs come from. Whether societal, familial, or cultural, our worldview has the power to limit our minds to a one-size, one-way mentality.

As a white, upper-middle-class teenager, my experiences with diversity were somewhat sheltered and limited. In the summers, I had the opportunity to go on a service project with my church to rebuild homes in the Appalachian region. This experience helped change my perspective, opened my eyes to appreciating cultural differences, and hugely influenced my decision to become a social worker. My higher education and many social services sector jobs gave me opportunities to become more aware, educated, and informed of the ways my biases and judgments show up. My willingness and openness to acknowledge these limits and allow uncomfortable and vulnerable feelings have helped me connect more easily and develop working relationships with those who differ from me.

Appreciating Diversity Tip

When working or interacting with others who differ from you, it helps to acknowledge those differences with an openness and willingness to learn and grow from a richer perspective. Defensiveness and resistance to differences quickly shut down the communication, learning, and growth that come from diversity.

Nurturing Diversity Iceberg

Consider for a moment how you nurture diversity and the ways it shows up in your life by filling in the tip of the iceberg above water. In the chunk of ice below the waterline, fill in any fears, reservations, or biases that you have about nurturing diversity.

The Paradox for Confused Minds

*I am the wisest man alive, for I know one thing,
and that is that I know nothing.*

— COMMON PARAPHRASE FROM PLATO, *Apology*

The more I learn and understand the complexities of life, the more it seems that so many aspects of life exist on a spectrum or in a paradox. I sometimes find myself contradicting myself with clients in sessions. For example, when someone comes to me to find relief from anxiety, I frequently work with them to allow uncomfortable feelings and run toward what makes them anxious. Seems counterintuitive, right? Aren't I supposed to help them not feel anxious?

A paradox is defined as a "seemingly absurd or self-contradictory statement or proposition that when investigated or explained may prove to be well-founded or true." Paradoxes cause confusion because the logical mind tends to reject contradictions and incongruencies. So much in life doesn't make sense, and it seems like the more we give attention to it, the worse it gets. For instance, my dog often sneaks into the trash can while I am away at work. When coming home to a trash-strewn floor, I used to scold and engage my dog, unknowingly reinforcing his behavior. While he would look remorseful and want reassurance

that I still loved him, to my frustration, the bad behavior continued. One day, I simply ignored the trash and picked it up later, not giving any attention to my dog. After a few days of this, to my surprise, the behavior stopped. This illustrates how something that seems the opposite of what makes sense can actually be more effective. I thought that through scolding my dog, the behavior would stop. Instead, I just reinforced his unwanted behavior.

Paradoxes show up in many ways and help us conceptualize this crazy and complex thing called life. In my work as a therapist, I've learned a lot of paradoxes, including the fact that giving negative attention to behaviors you want to decrease actually increases the behavior — just like with my dog. Another paradox: the opposite of trust is control. The more we trust something, the less we need to control it. The more we control something, the less we trust it. Another paradox involves the fear of dying, which causes paralysis in living. In working with anxiety disorders, most fears of a catastrophic event have a fear of death at the core. Yet, anxiety causes a ruminating and paralyzing effect, halting life through avoiding situations, which is the opposite of living fully.

In my practice, I often treat people with anxiety. They tend to avoid experiencing anxiety by avoiding the situations that create fear. Let's examine this one more closely. Avoidance makes the anxiety worse or stick around longer, while exposure to the fearful situation allows for the anxiety to resolve or lessen. Allowing ourselves to stay in a stressful situation feels paradoxical to our instinct to avoid it. Our brains have a survival function that helps create safety and protection. Unfortunately, this part of the brain does not differentiate between a real or a perceived threat. At times, this survival mechanism kicks in, creating unnecessary anxiety, particularly when no threat really exists, just the perception of a threat. Take, for instance, someone who has a fear of driving over bridges. The anxiety can

Paradox Check

Do any of these paradoxes show up in your life?

- The more you fear something, the more you should face it.
- The more opportunities to fail, the more chances to succeed.
- You must be vulnerable to have a connection, but you can't trust everyone.
- Social media drives deeper disconnection.
- Avoiding anxiety makes it worse, while allowing the uncomfortable feeling can lessen it.
- Trying to be happier makes us more unhappy.
- Life changes are the only things that happen with certainty.

become so paralyzing that this person avoids driving altogether. Learning to overcome this anxiety involves allowing the feelings of fear through exposure. This feels counterintuitive to the survival part of the brain, which activates a fight-freeze-or-flee response and causes the avoidance of driving. The paradox of allowing uncomfortable feelings when our survival instinct screams to avoid something can feel unnerving. But the discernment in allowing the paradox helps us to adjust, find balance, and operate on a higher cognitive level.

Writers often use paradoxes in literature to convey the human condition and to bring attention to a character or situation that makes no sense. Paradoxes allow for deeper analysis and reflection through considering plot or character development. It seems that paradoxes allow for acceptance or at least tolerance of the crazy complexities of life.

Consider for a moment situations in your life that have not made sense. Often you can find a paradox in there. I believe paradoxes are universal truths that humans seek to understand, and perhaps there is no full understanding of life. See, that's a paradox right there!

Embracing the paradoxes in life allows for radical acceptance. At times this brings a sense of comfort in accepting that ultimately things don't always make sense, even when in suffering. While we often long for peace and tranquility in life, how boring it would be if everything did make sense. That would take away from this messy, wild journey called life that has ups and downs, suffering and joy, pain and love. Life can simply be too complex to make sense.

In what areas of your life does your fear cause you to become paralyzed or avoid situations? How rational is this fear? What could you tell yourself to help find balance?

The Onion Technique

To help clarify confusion and understand how you feel on a deeper level, try the onion technique. I often use it in counseling sessions to quickly get to a root issue or deeper meaning. It consists of taking a situation or event, asking "what does that mean," and then asking the same question of your answer, over and over. Imagine a child responding with "why?" to every explanation you give, or peeling back the layers of an onion to get to the core. The goal is not to come up with an essential truth — as you can see in the example, "I'm not good enough" is never true! Rather, the goal is to get at your core feeling so that you can deal with it.

EXAMPLE

Situation or Event:

My friend does not invite me to a party.

What does that mean?

She doesn't like me

What does that mean?

I must have done something wrong

What does that mean?

I must be annoying

What does that mean?

I'm not good enough

Situation or Event:

....

What does that mean?

What does that mean?

What does that mean?

What does that mean?

WEEK
43

Amends for Remorseful Hearts

Chronic remorse, as all the moralists are agreed, is a most undesirable sentiment. If you have behaved badly, repent, make what amends you can and address yourself to the task of behaving better next time. On no account brood over your wrongdoing. Rolling in the muck is not the best way of getting clean.

— ALDOUS HUXLEY, Foreword to *Brave New World*

Admitting our mistakes and flaws can feel vulnerable and difficult. A genuine apology with honesty and integrity requires accepting uncomfortable feelings. Defense mechanisms kick in to alleviate the unpleasant feelings of guilt and shame. Most people tend to avoid those feelings. When we know we have acted in a way that has hurt a loved one or gone against our values, an apology and remorse can prove healing for both parties.

Apologizing does not mean making excuses or justifications. The need to avoid uncomfortable feelings causes justification, rationalization, minimization, and other defenses that drive disconnection from others and ourselves. Adding "I'm sorry" to a sentence does not constitute an effective apology. Some people might disguise a weak apology with an "I'm sorry," followed by a justification for the misdeed. Properly and genuinely apologizing creates safety and an opportunity to repair damage in a relationship.

An appropriate apology consists of saying sorry, acknowledging the damage or why your actions were wrong, asking for forgiveness, and offering to repair or make up for the hurt or damage caused. Often it is important to allow the apology receiver space and time to process and accept an apology. Remember, your part is to offer the apology genuinely and effectively without justifying or explaining. While a conversation can happen later exploring the reasons for the behavior, it is not best to explore this when apologizing.

I recently had a humbling experience where my child became my teacher. We are all human and make mistakes, and even as a therapist knowing the "right" way to handle things, I screw up — a lot. In this particular event, I used humor to handle a challenging and uncomfortable situation, as I often do in a healthy way. I forgot, though, that while humor can help me, it can sometimes hurt when it is directed toward others, coming off as insensitive. When I was confronted with this, my immediate reaction involved projecting blame onto my teenage child for being too sensitive. Yikes, did those words really come out of my mouth?

My kids have always acted as little truth mirrors, reflecting valuable, though sometimes hard to hear, insight right back at me. In this event, my wise child taught me that my ostensibly positive intent for using humor doesn't matter in the face of the fact that I hurt a loved one's feelings. To repair the damage, I had to let go of the need to prove my point, be right, or defend myself, and just listen to understand. Learning and owning up to our flaws and mistakes, while humbling, allows for growth, healing, better boundaries, and healthier relationships.

Having an apology can bring closure to a situation. But what happens when we never receive an apology? I can think of three major times in my life when someone hurt me, and I never received a genuine apology. These stand out to me like a sore thumb and taught me the valuable lesson of learning to find closure on my own. Moving forward

Anatomy of a True Apology

I'm sorry for...   I was wrong because...

Will you forgive me?

(Accept the response you get. You did your part in apologizing authentically, and the recipient may need time. Don't overstep the boundary and manipulate or make the person accept.)

Here's how I will make it better or repair it in the future.

without an apology is important. It helps to know that many people have very strong or pathological defenses against apologizing, finding it impossible or being unwilling to offer closure. Or perhaps they are blocked from your life or have died, making an apology impossible. Moving forward from someone who has hurt you involves extending yourself grace and compassion.

The first step involves recognizing how you feel and what contributes to these feelings. Then offering self-validation through acknowledging the right to feel these emotions facilitates the closure process. Offering yourself kindness and gentleness by reminding yourself that you may not have deserved to be treated that way or considering the ways you may have contributed to a

situation allow for a full reflection to ensure you have done the internal work and avoided any of your own defenses. Moving on without an apology requires self-awareness and a willingness to feel uncomfortable feelings.

If you struggle to find validation within yourself, consider talking with a trusted and safe friend or a therapist. Working through your feelings allows for more understanding. Sometimes, it helps to have a supportive third party to assist in that process. Through it all, you will begin to realize your worth does not come from whether someone else validates your feelings or acknowledges the hurt they caused. It comes from within, and you had the power all along to find closure.

How to Find Closure Without an Apology

1. Talk to someone about your feelings to get support and validation.

2. Self-validate.

3. Shift perspectives. Recognize that the lack of an apology does not reflect on your worth. Recognize that this lack comes from the other person.

4. Practice self-care and self-soothing.

5. Release and let go. Give it to God or the universe, and don't carry it around with you.

Apology Letter

Think about a situation in which you made a mistake or did something that created feelings of guilt or shame. You might even want to make an apology to yourself. Consider including in your letter some or all of the elements from the Anatomy of a True Apology on page 193.

Dear ....

I am sorry for: ....

....

....

....

....

....

....

....

....

....

Love always,

....

WEEK 44

Traditions in Modern Times

I like narrative storytelling as being part of a tradition, a folk tradition.

— BRUCE SPRINGSTEEN, *Springsteen on Springsteen*

As we saw in a previous chapter, our families of origin hugely impact our formative years, both in positive and negative ways. Research shows that children thrive in environments with consistency and routine. By creating safety and familiarity, rituals allow traditions to pass down through generations, helping us honor our heritage and past.

As social creatures, humans desire and need connection for safety, protection, and diversity in the different roles required for survival. In this section, you will explore memories, traditions, and rituals that meant a lot to you in your family and growing up. Now, while family dinners or shooting fireworks might not seem like an important part of staying alive, connection with others is critical in creating a life of meaning, security, and adaptation.

Nostalgia, coming from the Greek word meaning homecoming and ache, creates a sentimental feeling for things in our past that hold happy associations. These nostalgic feelings typically evoke feelings of safety and comfort, albeit sometimes a bittersweet longing. Do you find it amazing how one smell or sound can instantly transport you back in time or evoke strong feelings? I can smell cut grass and gasoline and immediately create an image of my father on his riding lawn mower. To better understand how our senses impact our memory, let's look at the brain.

For a simplified, basic explanation, the sensory organs controlling the five senses (ears, eyes, skin, mouth, and nose) send sensory impulses through the thalamus to the cerebral cortex, a higher-functioning part of the brain responsible for interpretation and cognition. The cortex has different sections that help determine judgment about the senses — for instance, determining pain from a hot stove or the smell of sour milk. The thalamus relays this sensory information to different parts of the brain like the hippocampus, which stores memory, and the amygdala, which controls the emotional center of our brains. Interestingly, the one sense that seems to be directly linked to memory is the sense of smell, which bypasses the thalamus, directly plugging into an olfactory bulb that is connected right to the hippocampus and amygdala. This direct connection perhaps explains why smells can instantly trigger a memory and even emotion like nostalgia.

When discussing memories and nostalgia, further reflection on the importance of family traditions and rituals surfaces. Just as children often need routines and structure to create a sense of safety and belonging, so too do adults. Centering around cultural or religious beliefs, traditions and rituals allow for connection and safety. Creating a cohesive sense of family or tribal unity allows for a sense of protection and belonging, an important evolutionary function for adaptation and survival.

As social beings, humans are hardwired to come together in connected living environments. Nurturing traditions and rituals serves as a vehicle for enhancing comforting security and a sense of belonging through creating familiarity with deeply ingrained activities, events, or behaviors that often pass down through generations over time.

Sensory Memories

Our senses have a powerful way of bringing us back to our memories. For each of the five senses, think of something from your past. Consider focusing on pleasant memories rather than unpleasant triggers as you learn to nurture nostalgia.

Sight   Smell   Taste   Touch   Hearing

Different cultures honor different traditions or holiday celebrations that reflect their cultural values or faith. Creating a strong foundation and connection to history and evolution, traditions serve to identify with a greater cause, belief system, or way of life.

Traditions serve the function of creating cohesiveness and security and offer a vehicle for teaching cultural values and norms. Without traditions and rituals, our world would become less cohesive and perhaps more chaotic.

Cultural Traditions

Here are some common traditions from countries other than the United States, which is where most of my readers will hail from (perhaps including you!). Neither cultures nor countries are homogenous, and many Americans with roots in other countries may already practice some of these traditions. But for those unfamiliar, it is interesting and useful to see examples of how diverse and specific other traditions can be — just like your own.

INDIA: Wear a red sari or lehenga for wedding; for some regions in India practicing Hinduism, cows are considered scared and cannot be eaten

CHINA: Wear red for wedding, as this is good luck; giving red envelopes with money to celebrate the Chinese New Year

RUSSIA: When visiting someone's home, be sure to bring a small gift like flowers or chocolate; do not wear shoes inside, but instead put on indoor slippers

EGYPT: Step into a new home with your right leg first for prosperity; hospitality etiquette is very important, so when hosting any visitors, the host must at least greet the visitors by offering a drink like tea or a soda

BRAZIL: Carnaval happens before Lent and features festivals and parades; every Wednesday is a day to enjoy feijoada, which is a meal of beans, meat, and spices

Carrying On the Tradition

Think back to a time in your life when your family (or other group) engaged in specific rituals. These can come from a cultural, familial, or even religious perspective. You can also include rituals you have created in the present. For example, one for me is Sunday dinners. As a kid, family mealtime played a large part in my nurturing. As a working mom with teenagers, I am happy to have at least one meal a week where I cook, and we sit at the table together!

	How It Made You Feel	How You Carry On
Favorite holiday practices		
Birthday celebrations		
Season changes		
Religious practices		

WEEK
45

Family in a Disconnected World

In truth, a family is what you make it.
It is made strong [...] by the rituals you help
family members create, by the memories you share,
by the commitment of time, caring, and love
you show to one another, and by the hopes for the future
you have as individuals and as a unit.

— MARGE KENNEDY and JANET SPENCER KING, *The Single-Parent Family*

Through blood, adoption, marriage, or soul tribe, families create a network of people who support, protect, and love through connection, loyalty, and bonds. While families come in many forms, understanding our families' important role and impact on our lives is an important part of growth and self-awareness, leading to healthier relationships.

Our family of origin is the family we grow up with. Often, parents or caregivers provide a stable environment for the upbringing of children, providing basic needs like safety and shelter and a sense of belonging. Families create a place for growth and connection as a child learns to navigate the external world, eventually growing up and launching into their own independence. Our families impact us in many ways, from rituals, traditions, and beliefs to modeling

healthy or unhealthy communication, habits, coping mechanisms, and values. While some people grow up with loving and supportive families, others may have experienced intergenerational trauma, abuse, neglect, or substance abuse, creating chaos, upheaval, and interpersonal drama during their formative years.

Nurturing a sense of family helps create a support tribe, allowing for safety, protection, and love. This can come from our blood ties, adoption, kinfolk, or even close friends who have played a role in our life as family. No matter the kind, family is an important aspect to nurture in our lives.

Whom do you consider your family of origin? While the typical traditional nuclear model lies in a mother and father, we can appreciate a much richer diversity in families when we consider same-sex parents, single-parent homes, grandparents as caregivers, group homes, and foster care. Think about the significance of who raised you and how they shaped your values, beliefs,

and sense of self. Our family of origin experiences, even when traumatic, can largely impact our lives and shape us to make changes to break the intergenerational cycle of abuse or dysfunction by doing things differently.

Through the growing field of epigenetics, science has fascinatingly shown the connection between intergenerational trauma and cell differentiation affecting gene expression. Our ancestors' traumas have the power to literally shape us on a behavioral and chemical level due to the genetic expression and impact on their children and grandchildren. This

❀ My Origin Experiences ❀

What cultural beliefs and messages
have shaped you to this day from your heritage?

....

....

....

....

....

....

....

has big implications for large groups affected by social or political trauma, such as survivors of the Holocaust, slavery, and war.

Some people may find deeper meaning in a spiritual connection to their ancestors, knowing they come from something greater than themselves. Identifying with certain family members through time can create a sacred and spiritual kinship. Other people might enjoy the historical aspect of ancestry and family history. Have you ever done a DNA heritage analysis? Do you know much about your family lineage and stories?

In many ways, our family of origin lays the foundations for our identity, self-worth, personality development, and coping patterns. For example, consider Kevin Leman's work on birth order.[19] *The Birth Order Book* explains the connection between our birth order and personality traits, which impacts our interpersonal relationships, career choices, and parenting styles. Firstborn children have shown higher rates of perfectionism with a high focus on achievement and a fear of failure, while last-born children tend to be more spontaneous, charming, and, at times, manipulative. Middle children take on the peacekeeper and people-pleasing roles. They often feel left out and lost in the family order. Only children tend to become natural leaders and often have a maturity from not having to share adult attention with siblings. They tend to be conscientious and perfectionists.

Unfortunately, sometimes intergenerational patterns include dysfunctional dynamics like childhood abuse, domestic violence, and substance abuse. While genetics may be a contributing factor, often the children in these families develop different roles and personality characteristics as a result of the unhealthy dynamics. Let's examine these roles more closely—see if you recognize any of these roles or behaviors in your family dynamic.

The "hero child," or "golden child," excels and carries the success and pride of the family. They often get attention for their accomplishments and achievements. The "scapegoat" plays the role of the "problem child," often holding negative qualities and characteristics projected by others. The scapegoat can internalize these beliefs and act out negatively. The "comedian" helps to defuse seriousness and events that might cause conflict. Sometimes they play the role as the peacekeeper through using humor to alleviate tension. Finally, the "lost child" becomes invisible, detaching and disconnecting. The focus on the scapegoat and hero child causes the lost child to disappear and go unnoticed. Understanding these different potential roles can help make sense of repeating patterns into adult years. Recognizing the impact of internalized belief systems from our families of origin can help to foster increased awareness and healthy changes breaking down negative patterns.

Home Is
Where the Heart Is

Let's take a moment to consider
the ways family has impacted your life.

Whom did you grow up with as a child? How was your family different
or similar to others around you?

How has extended family (grandparents, cousins, aunts and uncles)
played a part in your upbringing? Do you notice any generational
patterns or cycles?

What comes to mind when you hear the word "family"?

What role does family play in your life? How has your family influenced
your values and beliefs?

Intuition in Fearful Minds

*Practice listening to your intuition, your inner voice;
ask questions; be curious; see what you see; hear what you hear;
and then act upon what you know to be true.
These intuitive powers were given to your soul at birth.*

— CLARISSA PINKOLA ESTÉS, *Women Who Run with the Wolves*

People often say, "Trust your gut." But have you ever struggled to discern the difference between gut intuition and anxiety-based fear?

Anxiety and fear lead to overthinking, which leads to stagnation and analysis paralysis. Spinning thoughts round and round in your head keeps you stuck on the never-ending merry-go-round of what-ifs and assumptions, causing an endless loop of anxiety. Overthinking and intellectualizing develop as defense mechanisms designed for safety, which may have proven necessary for protection in unsafe or traumatic situations. Over time, though, overthinking halts action, masks intuition, and blocks you from your true path.

Intuition comes from our amazing brain's ability to take in and process information, sometimes before cognition allows us to realize what has happened fully. It's almost as if incongruencies or discrepancies trigger deeper awareness before our logical brains have awareness. While anxiety happens quickly, intuition comes on more slowly, like a gentle nudging becoming louder and louder when ignored.

People talk about "trusting your gut," perhaps because anxiety and intuition really do impact our intestinal systems. Those butterflies in the stomach and signs of gastrointestinal distress come from chemical changes that happen in the body due to adrenaline and other hormones, creating a surge of blood flow to the heart, lungs, and larger muscle groups. Our survival instincts literally involve distinct gut sensations.

Intuition can also manifest as a nudging body sensation. Something might feel off, giving us that uh-oh feeling, or a little voice in the back of our head may tell us to be careful. Intuition isn't easily explained by science, at least not in the traditional sense. For simplicity and practicality purposes, though, exploring intuition can have huge implications for making decisions in our lives. Tuning in and listening to our bodies can prove powerful in nurturing intuition. Through meditation, spending time in nature, and simply slowing down, our ability to listen to our inner voice and body sensations allows for a deeper awareness and appreciation of our inner knowing.

Six Strategies to Stop Overthinking in Its Tracks

1. **Defuse, defuse, defuse.** Use a "So what?" or "Who cares?" thought. Don't spend time figuring out if the overthinking thought is true or not. That will keep you stuck!

2. **Ground yourself.** Come back to your body through mindfulness with your five senses, or try some physical activity like yoga.

3. **Look for the positive thoughts.** Imagine the what-if thought from a positive frame of reference. What if I succeed? Now stop there.

4. **Take action.** Even a small step toward whatever makes you scared can help.

5. **Express the fear.** Move toward connecting with your emotions, just for a moment. Try journaling, drawing, or music to tap into those feelings.

6. **Distraction helps.** Temporarily, if you find yourself unable to stop ruminating, bring your attention to something else. NOTE: Any distraction can become avoidance or escape if it is used too much.

Understanding intuition involves differentiating it from anxiety and fear-based responses. Here are some differences worth noticing.

Anxiety or Fear	Intuition
Quick and frantic	Slow and gentle
Relieved	Comfortable
Questioning yourself	Trusting yourself
No	Yes

Some call intuition the sixth sense. Interestingly, intuition can come in sensory form, paralleling our five physical senses. Some hear sounds (clairaudience) or see images (clairvoyance). Some experience emotions or body sensations (clairsentience). Some even smell things like smoke (clairalience) or taste things like food or metals (clairgustance). Sounds strange, and, depending on your beliefs, this might not resonate. Regardless, it's interesting to connect intuitive methods with our sensory abilities. No matter the explanation, it's worth exploring how our intuition shows up for each of us.

Learning to let go and release overthinking can feel scary. This does not involve acting without thinking, for that would become impulsiveness. Releasing overthinking means letting go of the need to overcorrect, over-function, overanalyze, and over-plan. Nurturing intuition involves combining helpful thinking while paying attention to our external and internal reality. Although it is difficult to control anything outside of ourselves, trusting our gut and listening to how our intuition catches our attention can point us in the direction of our dreams.

My Intuition

How does intuition show up for you? Some options include: just knowing, emotions, hearing a little voice, body sensations, and seeing images. Can you think of examples of times when you had intuitions in these forms?

Analysis Paralysis Flowchart

Consider something that you have some reservations or feel unsure about. Answer the following flowchart to help organize your thoughts and feelings. Notice any difference in intuitive responses versus anxiety-driven reactions.

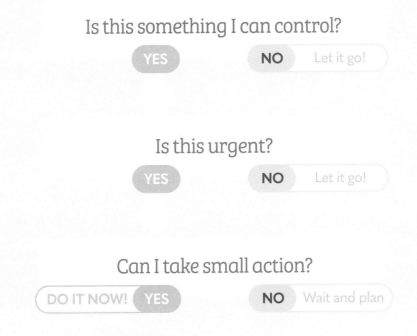

Is this something I can control?

YES   NO   Let it go!

Is this urgent?

YES   NO   Let it go!

Can I take small action?

DO IT NOW!   YES   NO   Wait and plan

Think about a situation where you listened to and trusted your intuition. What did you experience, and how did you respond? What signs did you notice that nudged you along?

Think about a time you ignored your intuition. What happened, and why did you ignore it?

Nurturing for Overextended Hearts

Love [is] the will to extend one's self for the purpose of nurturing one's own or another's spiritual growth. [...] Love is as love does. Love is an act of will — namely, both an intention and an action. Will also implies choice. We do not have to love. We choose to love.

— M. SCOTT PECK, *The Road Less Traveled*

Nothing makes more sense to include in a book about nurturing than how to nurture the nurturer! At times, the role of nurturer involves giving and prioritizing others' needs and wants before our own. It almost comes instinctively for mothers and other caregivers.

I can recall when my son, at six months of age, had a stomach virus, and I did too. I held and rocked him to give him comfort and then ended up throwing up all over his little head! This story always makes me smile when I think about how hard it can become to rest and self-nurture when responsibilities and parenting must happen. At times, practicing self-nurturing may feel impossible or counterintuitive, for nurturing implies an outward extension of energy, not inward toward ourselves.

Nurturing the nurturer doesn't mean to stop nurturing others; rather, self-nurturing means finding ways to replenish the energy reserves and fill our hearts with self-care and love to allow our light and kindness to extend to others. Taking on too much responsibility in nurturing others can lead to resentment and exhaustion.

Consider for a moment the ways others nurture you. This might prove difficult if you often find yourself in the nurturing role. I had to think hard on this one, but I came up with some answers. My animals nurture me unconditionally every day, greeting me with wiggle butts when I wake up, come home from work, or even come out of the bathroom. My father nurtures me through food; cooking allows him to tangibly show his love by ensuring our bellies are warm and full. How others nurture us can give us a clue on how best to nurture ourselves!

For me, spending an evening or weekend alone, time in nature, moving my body, or snuggling with my animals offers a healing nurturing deep within my soul. Daily, I nurture myself by practicing mindfulness, nightly meditation, and music. This recognition of self-care

Nurture Kit

In what ways do you nurture others? In what ways do you nurture yourself? Fill in the cup with ways you nurture yourself. Write words outside the cup with ways you nurture others.

practices becomes more powerful when moving beyond basic hygiene and eating, though these experiences can feel luxurious or cleansing too depending on the intention behind the action. Locking yourself in your bathroom with a bath bomb, candles, and soft music creates a whole new sensory and nurturing experience versus crossing off bathing on your to-do list.

Nurturing ourselves allows for recharging and reenergizing our emotional and spiritual battery. It is essential in allowing our light to shine in the world.

For some, self-nurturing might activate vulnerable feelings, especially in those who struggle to allow others to help them. As a highly independent person, I personally find it uncomfortable to need help or rely on others. For some reason, I have internalized accepting help as a weakness, which sounds ridiculous for someone dedicating her entire career to helping others. I always say it's easier to sit in my therapist's chair than on the proverbial sofa. In fact, accepting help, allowing others to nurture us, and permitting ourselves to self-nurture isn't weakness or selfishness at all. It ensures connection, reciprocity, and an endless supply of energy to refill our nurturing well to share in the world and with others.

Another component to nurturing the nurturer involves effective and healthy communication. Knowing how to and allowing ourselves to ask for help or communicate our needs creates a more wholehearted nurturing picture. Boundary-setting, like saying no or making a request and asking for help, allows us to bring our needs to the surface. Nurturing the nurturer must involve a balance in setting boundaries and a willingness to make requests and accept help from others. This nurturing balance creates the perfect formula for replenishing the energy reserves required for nurturing others.

❀ Nurturing the Nurturer ❀

How do you feel when others offer to help and nurture you in different ways? How can you ask for help or communicate your needs for nurturing more effectively?

Nurturing Pies

Consider ways that others nurture you and ways you extend nurturing to yourself. Draw your own pie chart using each empty pie, adding your own colors and labels and making each slice approximately the right size to reflect how big a role each aspect of nurturing plays in your life. Step back and look at your finished pies, and notice any areas of lack and any imbalances.

Ways Others Nurture Me

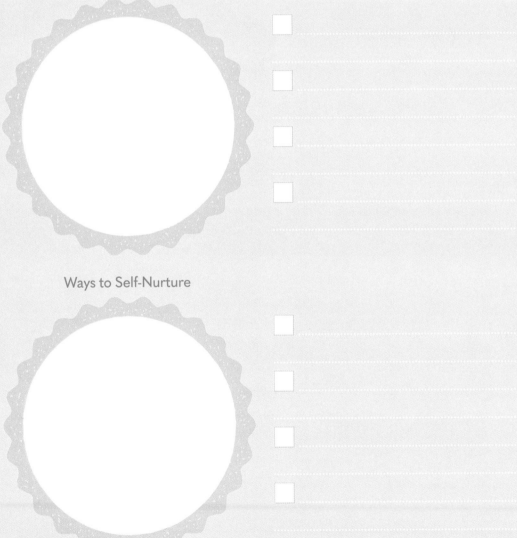

Ways to Self-Nurture

★ WEEK ★

48

Resilience Through Life's Struggles

*Life doesn't get easier or more forgiving;
we get stronger and more resilient.*

— STEVE MARABOLI, *Life, the Truth, and Being Free*

While beautiful and amazing, life can also be messy and filled with struggles and challenges. When dealing with grief and loss, trauma, disappointment, and forces outside of our control, resilience is a key component to surviving in our tumultuous world. Recovering from defeat, failure, and difficulties allows us to bounce back and try again. Learning ways to nurture resiliency helps us keep going when giving up sounds tempting. Focusing on learning life lessons allows for nurturing resiliency and wisdom.

I have held space for people who have endured unimaginable pain, from the tragic murder of a loved one, to horrific abuse in childhood, to betrayal from a deeply trusted family member. Time and time again over the years, I have watched with complete amazement how those same people can find healing moving forward in life. I have learned a lot about the strength of humans to endure such hardships and suffering and still create a life of meaning and hope. The ability for the human mind to recover and adapt allows for not just survival, but for living fully, even when experiencing unfathomable pain.

I have come to recognize some key components in people that allow for resiliency. These traits involve nurturing a sense of morality and values, a willingness and openness to fully experience deep emotions, intelligence and insight, flexibility, creativity in problem-solving, an openness to learning, and at times a sense of humor. These qualities allow for full healing through overcoming obstacles while living a life of meaning.

Humanity has become more and more resilient over time with environmental, medical, and technological advancements. Recognizing the external factors that contribute to resilience lets us see a more complete picture of where to focus our energy in bouncing back. Sometimes changing the environment allows for a more complete change to take place. Consider an addict in recovery. When completing a recovery program, an important consideration involves taking stock of environmental changes that might need to happen to ensure sobriety. Finding new friends, routines, or habits allows behavioral changes and reduces old triggers that might impact relapse. For those experiencing deep grief over the holidays, I often suggest a change in routine, like developing new traditions or giving permission to skip the holidays with a new scene. Changing our environment can help foster and support resiliency.

Another external consideration for nurturing resiliency involves examining our social supports and faith perspectives. Many individuals find comfort and peace through their faith-based beliefs that allow for meaning in life, even with suffering. While this might not ring true for everyone, a strong faith or belief system creates a foundation and context for protection, safety, and healing through meaning. A strong support system allows for a deeper connection to others and a communal sharing amidst suffering. Knowing others can hold space and offer support and comfort allows for strength in leaning upon another when feeling weak.

The internal process of nurturing resiliency involves developing strong self-awareness, a healthy dose of helpful thoughts, and implementing positive self-care practices. Knowing how to cope effectively with a balance of self-soothing, distraction, expressing

Finding Resilient Role Models

Consider someone whom you find to exemplify resilience. Think about what they have gone through and how they seem to have overcome obstacles. For example, I know of a family that lost a family member to homicide. They have embraced the idea of "feeding the good wolf" and fostering kindness and love, as opposed to hatred, in honor of their daughter — despite immense pain and grief.

feelings, and perspective-shifting creates a start to coping with resiliency. Remember, self-soothing involves nurturing the five senses when feeling uncomfortable emotions to provide comfort. Distraction techniques help shift our focus onto something else so that our emotions do not become destructive when we are suffering uncomfortable feelings. Learning ways to express feelings through the arts or sharing with a support system allows for processing difficult emotions rather than suppression of them. Perspective-shifting helps us find meaning amidst suffering through practicing gratitude, meditation, or prayer.

Psychological resiliency involves cognitive, behavioral, and environmental interventions. Helpful thoughts encourage realistic and positive thinking to help with adapting. This doesn't mean invalidating through toxic positivity but, rather, combines validation with a more helpful outlook. For a simple example, consider losing a wallet. A negative thought might sound like, "Just my luck. Nothing ever works out for me." A more resilient mindset sounds like, "Dang, I hate that I lost my wallet. What a pain. I guess I will have to cancel my credit cards, get a new driver's license, and look for a new wallet. In the grand scheme of things, this isn't the worst thing that could happen."

Nurturing Psychological Resilience

Think of an example for each kind of resilience given here. Think of a challenge or difficult situation you have or might encounter.

COGNITIVE
(how I think about the situation)

BEHAVIORAL
(things I can do to help the situation)

ENVIRONMENTAL
(things I can change in my surroundings)

Recipe for Resilience

Consider a struggle or challenge that has happened in your life or that you find yourself experiencing now. Share about this struggle and complete the recipe for resilience to help develop ways to nurture your ability to bounce back and keep moving forward. (An example recipe could be a recipe for a broken heart.)

A RESILIENCE RECIPE FOR:

2 cups of: ....

1 stick of: ....

1 tablespoon of: ....

½ teaspoon of: ....

A pinch of: ....

Add ingredients and blend together in a large, nurturing bowl. Grease a baking sheet lightly to allow negative things to slide off and not stick. Drop small spoonsful spaced out onto sheet. Allow time to bake at 350°F/175°C for at least 1 hour. Enjoy the sweet taste of resiliency.

Anger for Our Inner Warrior

*You should be angry. You must not be bitter.
Bitterness is like cancer. It eats upon the host.
It doesn't do anything to the object of its displeasure.
So use that anger. You write it. You paint it.
You dance it. You march it. You vote it.*

— MAYA ANGELOU

Nurturing anger might sound contradictory. Anger often carries a negative association, as most people try to find ways to calm down angry feelings rather than nurture them. Yet listening to and allowing anger helps life become fuller and more authentic. Anger, like all emotions, has a purpose and function. A powerful emotion, anger fuels action and helps communicate boundaries or our needs. Anger toward injustice helps propel making changes and bonds us with those who share similar beliefs or values.

Anger gives us a chance to zoom in on situations that might prove unfair, unjust, or morally unacceptable. For those who have experienced victimization or loss, anger allows for healing. It is an integral part of trauma and grief work. Anger helps us move toward resolution and acceptance of situations. Suppressing anger causes issues to our health and can become displaced onto innocent people or situations. When talking with children about anger in play therapy sessions, I often explain that feelings are neither good nor bad. They come like waves in the ocean, and it is okay to feel angry if that anger is expressed in a healthy and constructive manner.

Rooted in survival as the fight mechanism in response to a threat, anger controls, energizes, and discharges, and, when released, can produce calmness. The fight response allows us to protect ourselves from attacks or predators and defend our boundaries by sharpening our sensory organs and the increased flow of adrenaline to our heart and lungs.

Nurturing anger allows for acknowledging and healthily expressing our feelings. When feelings become pushed down or displaced, problems in relationships and health emerge. When suppressed and not fully processed, anger becomes toxic. It contributes to health issues like high blood pressure, teeth clenching and grinding (bruxism), and headaches.

Often anger feels uncomfortable and overwhelming, particularly for those exposed to negative expressions of anger like violence as a child or adult. This suppression of uncomfortable feelings can create unhealthy aspects when connecting with others, such as not communicating our wants and needs, ineffective boundary-setting, people-pleasing, or shutting down by disconnecting from all emotions. Examining this suppression involves looking at what happens when experiencing anger. Do you find yourself biting your tongue, clenching your teeth or hands, tightening your muscles, or not breathing? How then do these emotions get expressed?

Consider ways passively communicating causes problems in expressing your preferences or needs. Passive-aggressive tendencies happen when someone does not feel able to express anger and resorts to manipulating others through playing the martyr or getting even with someone. People pleasers often have a hard time disappointing others. They tend to suppress any negative emotion like anger for fear of rejection. If you find yourself engaging in these dynamics, consider the situations that might trigger angry feelings and explore more helpful ways to communicate and express those feelings rather than avoidance.

For some people, managing anger becomes problematic when not handled effectively. Anger, in fact, feels more powerful than experiencing hurt or fear.

Three Purposes of Anger

1. Validates feelings
2. Communicates preferences and needs
3. Prompts action

For this reason, those who avoid feelings of shame sometimes default to anger and rage as secondary emotions. The connection between hurt and anger allows for a cycle to emerge. Someone becomes triggered with more vulnerable feelings like hurt or rejection and then acts out with anger. These reactions can cause destructive communication patterns and actions, creating more feelings of shame or guilt. This cycle then repeats endlessly, from a triggering hurtful event or interpretation of an event to acting out of anger and back to feelings of hurt, shame, or rejection.

A better understanding of anger can emerge by identifying triggers and situations that create feelings of hurt, fear, or rejection. In working with clients learning anger management skills, recognizing the meaning and interpretation of events and neutralizing meaning can empower a more appropriate response. Identifying ways to calm down through restructuring or refocusing thoughts or attention can help. Recognizing the early body signals contributing to anger and knowing the urges that come with those reactions help allow for an alternative response like deep breathing, meditation, or redirecting (a healthier way to discharge feelings like exercise, music, or venting to a friend).

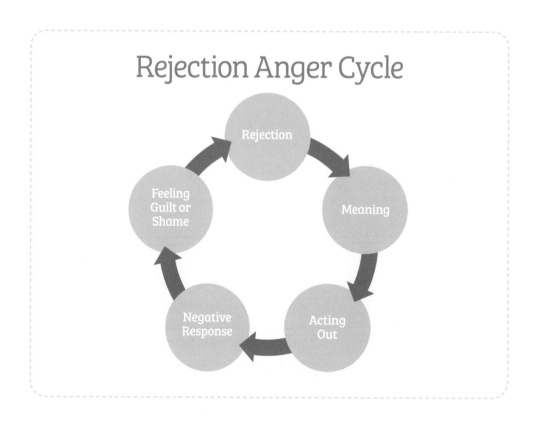

Rejection Anger Cycle

Rejection

Meaning

Acting Out

Negative Response

Feeling Guilt or Shame

Anger Triggers and Responses

First, list some situations, people, or events that you know trigger feelings of anger. For example, bullying or injustice.

Then, in the space below, describe or draw how you typically express anger and how others know you feel angry. Consider both healthy and unhealthy aspects of communication, like passivity, passive-aggressiveness, or aggressiveness.

Healing for Grieving Hearts

You will be whole again, but you will never be the same.
Nor should you be the same, nor would you want to.
— ELISABETH KÜBLER-ROSS and DAVID KESSLER, *On Grief and Grieving*

In all her glory, as the trees begin to lose their leaves and the sunlight fades among the chilly air, autumn gracefully teaches us about the painful process of letting go. Grief and loss are an unavoidable and inescapable part of life.

Healing from grief can feel painful and overwhelming and happens best in the context of nurturing emotions, connections with others, and finding meaning. By allowing a pathway to express our love and honor the changes in our life, grief validates the loss and hole in our hearts. Sitting with a parent who has lost a child or someone experiencing a sudden tragic loss, or supporting someone through the many continual losses that come from a chronic terminal illness like dementia, is a profound and almost sacred experience. Healing must happen through grief, not around, over, or under it.

Experiencing grief can come from other losses besides death, too, like losing a job, a divorce or relationship breakup, or relocation. Losses can happen in conjunction with happy situations like retirement or going to college. Nurturing healing involves normalizing and allowing the full feelings of grief and loss that come with those changes.

Grief work is just that — work. It does not happen magically, and it involves a conscious awareness of emotions and storytelling of the past and present as a new reality takes shape. It helps to know that the feelings and stages of grief are normal and necessary for healing. Elisabeth Kübler-Ross, a pioneer in the field of death and dying, shared the most helpful conceptualization and study of grief through identifying universal stages.[20] Through the stages of shock and denial, bargaining, anger, depression, and eventually acceptance, grief does not happen linearly but seems to ebb and flow between stages like the changing tides.

In healing from grief and loss, it is important to examine and challenge certain myths (see the sidebar on page 222). Often these myths state rigid rules that create a feeling of pathology and judgment. Remember too that it is impossible to tell someone else how to grieve, for there is no right or wrong way. Every person handles emotions differently and finds individualized ways to cope and process the loss in whatever time frame happens for them.

Five Things I've Learned about Grief as a Therapist

1. **Grief hurts.** I mean, physically hurts. Your lungs when you can't breathe. Your heart when it breaks in two. Your eyes when they swell and burn from salty tears.

2. **Grief spirals.** The grieving process is not linear. It goes around and around like one of those crazy spinning playground roundabouts. Sometimes you can't get off even when you try, and your grief seems stuck and won't budge.

3. **Grief happens.** There's no way around it. We all lose someone near and dear to our hearts at some point. Some pass tragically and unexpectedly. Some fight the long, hard battle. Either way, you are never really prepared.

4. **Grief changes you.** Fundamentally, at your core. Things that used to matter simply don't anymore. You gain a new perspective of what it means to live with a hole in your heart.

5. **Grief heals.** Over time, healing happens as you learn to accommodate your world without your loved one. Time doesn't heal grief. You don't get over it or around it, just through time passing. You can try to numb and escape it, but it never goes away. You eventually learn to grieve and heal the broken parts of your heart.

Common Myths about Grief

1. **Certain kinds of loss are worse,** like a sudden death versus death after a long illness. No one type of loss is worse.

2. **Time heals all wounds.** This is not true. Healing heals all wounds by allowing the grief to happen; feeling emotions allows for grief to become fully expressed and processed.

3. **You should be over it in a year.** There is no time frame for getting over grief. It does take time and work to process the many changing emotions and eventually reach acceptance and accommodation.

4. **Once you've grieved, you're done.** Grief comes in waves and attacks depending on the season, anniversary dates, or special occasions. Grief can hit out of nowhere. It can happen just as intensely and profoundly as when first experiencing the pain.

5. **The right way to grieve is…** There is no right or wrong way to grieve. Some choices might prolong the grief through destructive or numbing behaviors to avoid uncomfortable feelings. But the grieving process is neither right nor wrong.

6. **Talking or crying about grief makes it worse.** This couldn't be further from the truth. Talking and processing our loss, while painful and heartbreaking, allows for a more complete resolution. Grief hurts worse when suppressed and avoided.

7. **I should be stronger and not bother anyone with my grief.** The idea that grief brings others down and should stay hidden inhibits healing and processing. Find those who support you.

8. **I can't live life and be happy, or it will mean I didn't really love my person.** Learning to accommodate life without a loved one can feel counterintuitive and bring up feelings of misplaced guilt. Although the deceased is no longer here, our lives continue, and most deceased loved ones would want us to live fully.

My Grief Story

In the space below, share a loss you've experienced and how you found ways to honor your experiences through your grief story. Consider ways you honored your past and how you processed your emotions.

My grief story involves:

....

....

....

A way I honored my loved one or my loss involved:

....

....

....

A ritual I participated in that gave me strength:

....

....

....

During anniversaries of certain dates, I find myself:

....

....

....

Something I have learned through my grief is:

....

....

WEEK 51

Wisdom for Evolving Souls

Wisdom ceases to be wisdom when it becomes
too proud to weep, too grave to laugh,
and too self-ful to seek other than itself.

— KAHLIL GIBRAN, *Sand and Foam*

For the last two mind-blowing, heart-expanding decades, I have sat in the therapist's chair, clocking well over two hundred thousand hours, humbly listening to the intimate details of others' suffering and struggles. My clients' stories have given me insight that transcends my own personal experiences or education.

In that time, I've become intimately connected and interwoven into people's inner worlds. Through our tears, our laughter, and our heavy silences, I have gained invaluable wisdom from them through my special privilege as a therapist. These are not my stories. This is not my wisdom. It is the collective wisdom that comes from the resiliency of the human spirit and the sacred work that happens in a counseling session. I can think of no greater honor.

Nurturing wisdom comes from allowing inner reflection, noticing the world around us, and an openness to learning

lessons. The power and richness that come from making connections or realizing universal truths in life through our own or others' experiences give us a complete awareness and a new level of transcendence from emotional pain and suffering. Wisdom comes from honoring truth even when it is hard to hear and uncomfortable to speak.

Life lessons teach us new ideas and give a different perspective, helping us evolve and grow, an important component of wisdom. Just learning information through books or formal education doesn't allow for true wisdom. The insight comes from experiences, mine or yours. Wisdom does not have to come from hardship, misery, and suffering. However, these can give us a glimpse into resiliency and a more complete understanding of life's complexities.

Wisdom is something to be cultivated throughout life, not a final goal to be reached near the end of life. And it is a two-way street from any one person and any one generation to another. Each person, whether adult, teen, or child, must learn through their own journeys. But each person must simultaneously understand that they can learn from others' journeys by listening and validating — not by being lectured, but by hearin g the personal wisdom of others from the unique lives those others have led.

Think about yourself as a teenager. Surely, you've grown, matured, and have a different perspective now as an adult. As a mother of teenagers, I have found that my wisdom, while I believe it to be brilliantly true, might not prove beneficial, relevant, or wanted to my children. I can sometimes act as a guide to help steer them along the way, but still, as they grow in their wisdom, and I grow in mine, I've found that both my children, at ages sixteen and seventeen, sometimes have more wisdom than my forty-five-year-old self.

We each have our own individual wisdom and experience shaping who we are and the legacy we pass down to younger generations and on to others. This idealism has roots in our cultural and religious background. It is important to consider our cultural values, because what might seem wise in one country might appear foolish in another.

Historically, before the modern age, wisdom focused on the supernatural and transcendence into the divine and moral arena. Over time, the Western world adapted developmental psychology with Piaget's stages of child development and Erikson's psychosocial

Timelines and Lessons

Consider the following developmental stages in your life.
What lessons did you learn, even the hard way? If you haven't reached
a certain stage, consider interviewing someone in that stage.

- Childhood
- Adolescence
- Young adulthood
- Midlife
- Golden years

stages to combine knowledge and cognition as synonymous with wisdom in helping to change and influence the environment to solve problems. In the Western world, therefore, wisdom often relies on obtaining knowledge through analytical reasoning. The Eastern conceptualization of wisdom pulls on Confucianism, Buddhism, and Taoism and focuses more on the inherent moral aspects of wisdom with a combination of benevolence and intelligence for inner awareness, enlightenment, and harmony.[21] It is important to consider the diversity in life experiences and hardships, as well as cultural implications, for a full understanding of the conceptualization of wisdom.

Hacks for Nurturing Wisdom

1. Try new things and meet new people. Diversity allows for a richer and fuller awareness of different perspectives.

2. Listen to others share their stories and note the lessons they have learned.

3. Take risks and release the fear of failure. Making a mistake allows growth and learning, a key component of gaining wisdom.

4. Find meaning in things that don't make logical sense and embrace the paradoxes in life.

5. Search for and speak your truth.

Tips for
Living Life Wisely

We all have wisdom inside of us worth sharing. Create a list of things
you have learned about life and want to share with others.

Endings for New Beginnings

October knew, of course, that the action of turning a page, of ending a chapter or of shutting a book, did not end a tale. Having admitted that, he would also avow that happy endings were never difficult to find: "It is simply a matter," he explained to April, "of finding a sunny place in a garden, where the light is golden and the grass is soft; somewhere to rest, to stop reading, and to be content."

— NEIL GAIMAN, *The Sandman, Volume 4: Season of Mists*

Just as fall relinquishes her fight to the winter chill, we come to the final week in this workbook, a perfect time to reflect on endings and new beginnings. After sharing such deep intimacy with clients, I have always found goodbyes hard as a therapist. In the clinical world, we call this termination, but I refuse to use that word, given the abruptness and finality of its meaning.

Over the years, I've learned that endings in therapy become a natural part of the therapeutic process, allowing for evolution and growth, not finality. While my part in someone's journey may end, life continues to flow with new beginnings. When working with children and saying goodbye, I explain that my heart simply gets bigger with more compartments to keep each child's memory inside. While endings evoke feelings of sadness and loss, they truly open the door to the beginning of something new. Just as the seasons change with each earthly rotation around the sun, life follows suit, creating an unending circle of endings and new beginnings.

Nurturing endings creates an opportunity for reflection on life experience. Hospice social workers

Turning Endings into New Beginnings

Think about an ending in your life and how this created a path for a new beginning. I'll give an example from my life to inspire you.

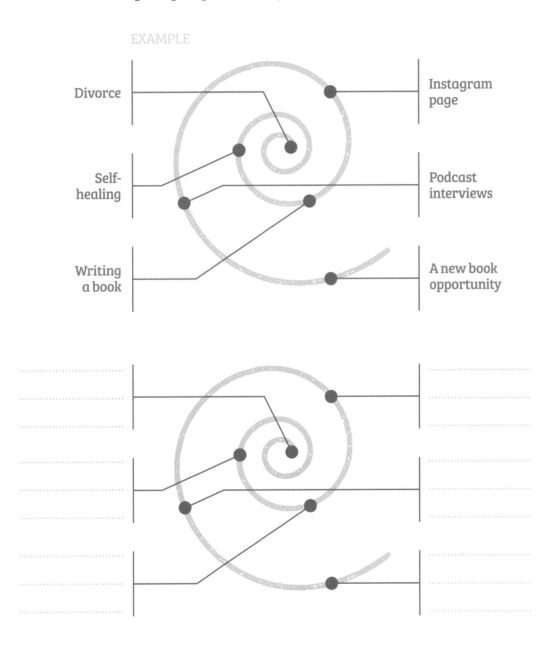

Divorce

Instagram page

Self-healing

Podcast interviews

Writing a book

A new book opportunity

call this deep reflection a life review. Reflecting on previous events and experiences in life helps prepare for the end. It opens the way for a peaceful transition into a new realm. Depending on your belief system, for those who have a spiritual mindset, facing the final ending of human life brings forth a new beginning on the soul level. For those of a more scientific mindset, energy can be neither created nor destroyed, calling for the renewal of energy in a different form.

Nurturing endings must involve reflecting on hidden aspects of things unseen and unknown. Think about endings in your life that at the time felt heartbreaking, something you might never get over. I can recall once getting turned down for a job I wanted, only to stumble across something better that allowed me to start my own private practice. The ending of my seventeen-year marriage allowed me to reconnect with myself and embark on a self-love journey, opening the doors to writing a book. Endings bring new life and new opportunities.

An important aspect in nurturing endings involves reflecting on the lessons learned as that chapter closes. Before writing the next chapter, deep inner reflection will prove helpful to properly reconcile and make peace with the past, adding a richness of content in writing your next story. Often, reflecting on regrets or mistakes offers invaluable information on making changes or doing things differently. Openness to experiencing endings with grace and introspection lays the pathway to enlightenment and enrichment.

Sometimes endings come from a place of willingness and choice. Other times endings happen without our consent. Goodbyes create painful emotions that call for healing and nurturing, no matter the situation. Nurturing the goodbyes in life involves honoring your story, your truth, and your lessons fully and completely. Through exploring your triumphs and successes, knowing your gifts and strengths, and building on areas to grow and improve, endings become new beginnings in the best possible way. When this work does not happen, cycles often repeat, with similar opportunities to learn the lesson.

As this last chapter brings us to the end of our nurturing work together, hopefully you have gained insight and inspiration and intend to create continued nurturing throughout your life journey. Exploring the many angles connected to nurturing allows for deeper self-reflection and awareness, opening to a healing space to find answers that already exist within you. This book just scratches the surface of many concepts like forgiveness, values clarification, and creativity, to name a few. This is a therapeutic workbook with roots in evidence-based approaches, and the assessments and activities in it come anecdotally and from my experiences as a therapist, not as a researcher or professor. I strongly encourage you to delve deeper into exploring many of these topics further. (And please check out the book's Resources and Further Reading section for a wonderful list of resources for your continued self-nurturing work.)

The time you have spent nurturing over these fifty-two weeks will hopefully propel you on a new beginning for an even deeper connection with yourself, others, and the world around you as you continue to search for nurturing opportunities. At times you might consider revisiting parts of this workbook that deeply resonate or call you back as perspectives shift and your growth matures; or perhaps you will decide to start or join a book club on your quest for nurturing connections.

You deserve a huge congratulations for your openness and willingness to embrace healing and nurturing from a complete mind, body, spirit perspective. I truly honor your work and feel so blessed and grateful you have chosen this workbook to accompany you on your nurturing quest. May you continue to grow through the seasons of your life, filled with love and nurturing for your unique self.

❧ What I've Learned ❧

What will you take along with you from the introspection
and reflection done in this book?

....

....

....

....

....

....

My Nurturing Experience

For our final exercise, let's assess your views on nurturing and how you have learned to be kind to yourself, and consider how you have grown in your work through this book. Reflect on each of the below statements in detail, flipping back through this book to reference the exercises you've already completed if desired.

1 I recognize new ways for me to nurture my mind, body, and spirit.

....
....
....

2 Nurturing has become a regular part of my daily or weekly routine.

....
....
....

3 I am open to nurturing all aspects of my life and the world around me.

....
....
....

4 I have a new appreciation of what it means to nurture myself fully.

....
....
....

5 I realize that nurturing happens in ways beyond self-care.

....
....
....

6 I embrace my divinity and inner gifts and know how to share
   them in the world.

   ....
   ....
   ....

7 Nurturing myself means I can extend nurturing to others.

   ....
   ....
   ....

8 I hope to share this book with others in need of nurturing.

   ....
   ....
   ....

9 The concept of nurturing through the four seasons resonates
   with my journey.

   ....
   ....
   ....

10 Nurturing involves intention and hard work.

   ....
   ....
   ....
   ....
   ....
   ....

Resources and Further Reading

Completing a workbook can create inspiration and unlock a desire for continued growth in areas that might need more attention. Here are some resources for different topics to help you dig deeper into your continued self-love journey.

Nurturing the Mind

Brené Brown has written several books that talk about the importance of embracing vulnerability, expressing feelings, and living authentically. She also has a powerful Tedx Talks video about the power of vulnerability.

- *The Gifts of Imperfection* (2010)
- *Daring Greatly* (2015)
- *Rising Strong* (2017)
- *Atlas of the Heart* (2021)

Kristen Neff, PhD, an early adopter in the self-compassion arena, has several excellent books and courses for those who want to explore the topic further. Her website offers helpful guided meditations, assessment tools, and exercises to incorporate into a self-compassion practice.

- *Fierce Self-Compassion: How Women Can Harness Kindness to Speak Up, Claim Their Power, and Thrive* (2021)
- *Self-Compassion: The Proven Power of Being Kind to Yourself* (2015)
- Self-Compassion.org, *https://self-compassion.org*

Lori Gottlieb, a psychotherapist and bestselling author, offers a brilliant glimpse into the experience of talk therapy from both the perspective of a therapist and a patient. Candid and touching, her story shares the power behind our humanness. She also has a workbook to accompany her bestselling book.

- *Maybe You Should Talk to Someone: A Therapist, HER Therapist, and Our Lives Revealed* (2019)

- *Maybe You Should Talk to Someone: The Workbook: A Toolkit for Editing Your Story and Changing Your Life* (2021)

Lucia Capacchione's work highlights the creative and unique technique of nondominant hand journaling to help connect with and heal the inner child.

- *Recovery of Your Inner Child: The Highly Acclaimed Method for Liberating Your Inner Self* (1991)

Viktor E. Frankl, a Nazi concentration camp survivor and the father of logotherapy, writes about finding purpose and meaning even amidst life's suffering.

- *Man's Search for Meaning: An Introduction to Logotherapy* (1962)

Louise Hay has created numerous materials highlighting self-esteem and self-help for your nurturing journey.

- *You Can Heal Your Life* (1987)
- *How to Love Yourself: Cherishing the Incredible Miracle That You Are* (2005)

Shauna Shapiro, PhD, a bestselling author, clinical psychologist, and expert in mindfulness and self-compassion, has several inspiring books, videos, and journals to help you along your nurturing journey.

- *Good Morning, I Love You: Mindfulness and Self-Compassion Practices to Rewire Your Brain for Calm, Clarity, and Joy* (2020)

The following free **classic assessment tools** offer helpful and validating information on how experiencing different life events can impact stress levels.

- The Holmes-Rahe Stress Inventory (1967), *https://www.stress.org/holmes-rahe-stress-inventory*
- The Perceived Stress Scale (1994), *https://das.nh.gov/wellness/docs/percieved%20stress%20scale.pdf*

Nurturing the Body

A motivational speaker and body positivity warrior, **Harnaam Kaur** shares her story of self-love and inspires others on their journey.

- *http://harnaamkaur.com*

This website helps you consider your **sleep cycles** and calculates the optimal time to fall asleep to ensure waking refreshed.

- *https://sleepyti.me*

A wonderful way to nurture the mind, body, and soul includes **incorporating yoga** into a regular practice. Whether in the form of following online videos, doing yoga in the studio, or practicing on the beach, this can become a wonderful way to de-stress, move your body, and connect with your spiritual self. I have found yoga and meditation teacher **Yely Rivas-Staley of Yoga Yely** to be a wonderfully nurturing resource on many levels. And she is bilingual (in English and Spanish)!

- *www.yogayely.com*; Instagram: @yogayely

Nurturing the Spirit

Religion and faith-based practices offer people meaning and purpose as well as connection throughout the world. While religion has roots in faith and spirituality, ongoing research and academic efforts help explore the science behind consciousness and life after death. Here are some interesting resources to check out.

- Information about the major religions of the world: *https://www.infoplease.com/culture-entertainment/religion/major-religions-world*
- Evidence-based research on consciousness, life after death, and perceptual studies by the University of Virginia, School of Medicine, Psychiatry Department, Division of Perceptual Studies: *https://med.virginia.edu/perceptual-studies*

Nurturing the World Around Us

A wonderful way to support the world around us involves learning more about conservation and the environment. These nonprofit organizations help offer education and opportunities for social and environmental justice and action.

- The Nature Conservancy, *https://www.nature.org*
- The Sierra Club, *https://www.sierraclub.org*

References

1. "Feng Shui." National Geographic Society Resource Library. https://www.nationalgeographic.org/encyclopedia/feng-shui.

2. Cherry, Kendra. "Color Psychology: Does It Affect How You Feel?" Verywell Mind. https://www.verywellmind.com/color-psychology-2795824.

3. "Marketing Psychology of Colors: The Importance of Color Meaning." Swift Publisher. https://www.swiftpublisher.com/useful-articles/psychology-of-colors.

4. Sifton, Elisabeth. *The Serenity Prayer: Faith and Politics in Times of Peace and War.* New York: W. W. Norton, 2003.

5. Mogi, Ken. *The Little Book of Ikigai: The Essential Japanese Way to Finding Your Purpose in Life.* London: Quercus Editions, 2017.

6. Winn, Marc. "What Is Your Ikigai?" The View Inside Me. http://theviewinside.me/what-is-your-ikigai.

7. "Butterfly Life Cycle." Academy of Natural Sciences of Drexel University. https://ansp.org/exhibits/online-exhibits/butterflies/lifecycle.

8. "Perceived Stress Scale." State of New Hampshire Employee Assistance Program. https://das.nh.gov/wellness/docs/percieved%20stress%20scale.pdf; and "The Holmes-Rahe Stress Inventory." American Institute of Stress. https://www.stress.org/holmes-rahe-stress-inventory.

9. Capacchione, Lucia. *Recovery of Your Inner Child: The Highly Acclaimed Method for Liberating Your Inner Self.* New York: Simon & Schuster, 1991.

10. Brooks, Arthur C. "The Meaning of Life Is Surprisingly Simple." *The Atlantic.* https://www.theatlantic.com/family/archive/2021/10/meaning-life-macronutrients-purpose-search/620440.

11. Beck, Aaron T., A. John Rush, Brian F. Shaw, and Gary Emery. *Cognitive Therapy of Depression.* New York: Guilford, 1979.

12. Brown, Brené. "The Power of Vulnerability." TED. https://www.ted.com/talks/brene_brown_the_power_of_vulnerability

13. Gibran, Kahlil. *The Prophet.* Richmond, UK: Alma Classics Evergreen, 2020.

14. Becker, Gavin de. *The Gift of Fear.* London: Bloomsbury, 2000.

15. Murrah, Jeff. "The Etymology of Passion." Owlcation. https://owlcation.com/humanities/The-Etymology-of-Passion.

16. Linehan, Marsha M. *DBT® Skills Training Manual 2nd ed.* New York: Guilford, 2015.

17. Netherlands Organization for Scientific Research. "Half of Your Friends Lost in Seven Years, Social Network Study Finds." *ScienceDaily.* www.sciencedaily.com/releases/2009/05/090527111907.htm

18. "Friendships: Enrich Your Life and Improve Your Health." Mayo Foundation for Medical Education and Research. https://www.mayoclinic.org/healthy-lifestyle/adult-health/in-depth/friendships/art-20044860

19. Leman, Kevin. *The Birth Order Book: Why You Are the Way You Are.* New York: Dell, 1992.

20. Kübler-Ross, Elisabeth, and David Kessler. *On Grief and Grieving: Finding the Meaning of Grief through The Five Stages of Loss.* New York: Scribner's, 2005.

21. Wang, Zhen-Dong, Yi-Meng Wang, Kang Li, Juan Shi, and Feng-Yan Wang. "The Comparison of the Wisdom View in Chinese and Western Cultures." *Current Psychology* (2021). https://doi.org/10.1007/s12144-020-01226-w.

Group Guide

How to Use This Workbook with Others

This book offers a wonderful way to connect and nurture others when shared with your tribe! Consider starting or joining a virtual or in-person book club or even organizing a retreat. Here are some tips for sharing your nurturing journey with others.

1. **Embrace vulnerability.** Work to have a willingness and openness to show up authentically.

2. **Decide on a format.** Consider taking one season at a time to reflect and share with others about the narrative portions and your responses for different exercises from that season. Pick the activities or messages that speak to you.

3. **Consider the time frame for meeting.** If meeting weekly for an entire year is unrealistic, consider meeting monthly or even for a limited time frame like eight weeks. You could pick two chapters from each season. Invite participants to share their favorite activity or message.

4. **Encourage others to embrace imperfection.** Sometimes showing up even if you haven't completed the exercises fully can prove inspiring and offer valuable support and insight. Don't add extra pressure to have completed every single thing.

5. **Embrace diversity.** For a richer experience, consider inviting those who differ from you to your group for deeper reflection and understanding.

6. **Work around barriers.** Find ways to help include others who might not feel comfortable participating by choosing virtual or other methods for connecting. If some are feeling anxious about being seen, invite them not to use their videos if gathering virtually.

7. **Create an expectation about participation.** To encourage intimacy and safety, have members commit to participating regularly, only missing when necessary. Also decide if your group is open or closed. An open group involves members dropping in and coming and going, sometimes with new people participating. A closed group keeps the group limited to only those who sign up initially. A closed group allows for safety and cohesiveness, and an open group allows for reaching more people.

8. **Use a facilitator.** Have a leader to keep the group on track and running smoothly. This encourages equal participation and keeps the group focused and moving along.

9. **Add a structure.** Consider developing a structure to have the same format each week, whether that's sharing a quote, checking in with others, or having a closing ritual. This helps create cohesiveness and familiarity.

10. **Embrace flexibility.** While structure does have benefits, allowing the group to create its own flow leaves room for spontaneity and the magic of connection.

Index

BETTER DAY BOOKS®

HAPPY · CREATIVE · CURATED

Business is personal at Better Day Books. We were founded on the belief that all people are creative and that making things by hand is inherently good for us. It's important to us that you know how much we appreciate your support. The book you are holding in your hands was crafted with the artistic passion of the author and brought to life by a team of wildly enthusiastic creatives who believed it could inspire you. If it did, please drop us a line and let us know about it. Connect with us on Instagram, post a photo of your art, and let us know what other creative pursuits you are interested in learning about. It all matters to us. You're kind of a big deal.

it's a good day to have a better day!®

www.betterdaybooks.com
better_day_books